Toby

The
cross-eyed
stray

Celia Haddon

hamlyn

To Ronnie, who never read my books anyway.

Copyright © Octopus Publishing Group Ltd 2015

Text copyright © Celia Haddon 2015

ISBN 978-0-600-63098-2

A CIP catalogue record for this book is available from the British Library

Printed and bound by CPI Group (UK) Ltd, Croydon, CR0 4YY

10 9 8 7 6 5 4 3 2 1

Contents

Sleep on my love

Sleep on, my love, in thy cold bed
Never to be disquieted!
My last good-night! Thou wilt not wake
Till I thy fate shall overtake;
Till age, or grief, or sickness must
Marry my body to that dust
It so much loves; and fill the room
My heart keeps empty in thy tomb.
Stay for me there, I will not fail
To meet thee in that hollow vale.
And think not much of my delay:
I am already on the way,
And follow thee with all the speed
Desire can make, or sorrows breed.
The thought of this bids me go on,
And wait my dissolutiòn
With hope and comfort. Dear (forgive
The crime) I am content to live
Divided, with but half a heart,
Till we shall meet and never part.

This is part of a longer poem, *Exequy on his Wife*,
by Henry King, 1592–1669

Chapter 1

The cat living under a car

The small, thin, bedraggled ginger cat was standing at the bottom of the garden. He looked frozen with fear and, somehow, at the same time desperate for love. He was obviously poised for flight, ready to run if a human were to shout at him or throw a stone. Yet if cats could speak, this cat was pleading: 'Help me.'

Everything about him suggested a cat at the limits of his endurance. His ginger coat looked pale and faded, as if the orange was leaching from his fur. Although his mouth and whiskers were white, they were a very dirty white. A dingy ruff of fur round his neck was tangled and thin. His tail was fluffy but it hung downwards as if he hadn't the strength to raise it.

He was hungry, starving even. Longingly, he eyed the scraps of cat food that Gaynor had put out in her garden under a bench for the local hedgehogs. This was the food that

Gaynor's own well-fed cats had rejected or just not got around to eating.

For a few minutes he just hovered there at the end of the garden, directing his gaze towards the bowl. Then, as if he had had to gather all his courage to make a move, he walked cautiously towards it. With an anxious look around to see if he was observed, he thrust his face into the bowl and gobbled up all the food. Then he retreated fast to the relative safety of the shrubs without pausing to wash himself.

'He was absolutely ravenous that day,' said Gaynor. She was watching him through her conservatory windows, being careful not to let him see her.

'He's back again,' Gaynor said to her mother the next day as they looked through the same windows into the garden. The ginger stray was hanging around and today he had moved a little closer to the house. He was obviously waiting. This time, he looked straight at her and miaowed hopefully.

'I'll put out some more food.' She went out and put down a bowl of fresh cat food on the paving near the house wall. The ginger cat retreated to the shrubs as she emerged but as she went back inside the house, he moved to the bowl and ate with a desperate appetite. At the end of his meal, bolder than on the last occasion, he licked the bowl very carefully and thoroughly from bottom to top. Every single fragment of food accounted for, he retreated to the shrubs again at the bottom of the garden. This time he sat upright and licked round the edge of his mouth in case any small trace of food was left on his muzzle.

This wasn't the first time he had visited their garden. Gaynor's mother had caught sight of him before, coming over the wall and taking refuge in the shrubs. He had perhaps been trying to find shelter from the November rain; or maybe knew to wait there till nightfall, when the curtains were closed and Gaynor and her mother were safe inside, before coming out to investigate the hedgehogs' bowl in the hope they had left something for him.

Gaynor loves cats and local cats seem to know this. Even when she goes on holiday, a cat seems to turn up on the doorstep of any holiday flat she is renting. Perhaps some kind of secret mark, a pawmark or a scratch, has been left on her doorstep or on the nearby bushes, which says to other cats: 'Sucker lives here.'

A generation ago, tramps, travellers and beggars used to leave such a mark, made with a knife or sharp stone, on the door or the gatepost of friendly houses. It was a secret mark that ordinary people would not notice, but for others on the tramp, the mark showed that the household was good for a cup of tea, or possibly even some small change.

Perhaps the cats in Gaynor's neighbourhood had done the same, which is why this small ginger cat, so badly in need of his next meal, had turned up at her house on a well-kept private housing estate in the Cotswolds. Somehow he had known, or at least hoped, that he would get help there. 'Across the road from me there are farms and I think the farm cats sometimes come over here,' she says.

Gaynor already had a household of cats. Elderly Percy, at 18 years old a venerable ginger and white cat, presided magisterially over the two younger cats, tabby and white Lily and sleek black Indie. Lily and Indie had been rescued as feral kittens and were still a little shy of strangers. Unlike them, Percy was magnificently laid back with all human visitors.

'Everybody knew Percy,' recalls Gaynor. 'He would sit in our drive in the sun and walk out to greet the passing schoolkids.'

His preferred seat was on the windowsill from where he could watch human and feline passersby.

These were the three cats Gaynor owned, but there were others, too. Cats would look in at Gaynor's home while passing – just in case there was food going. Like the home of the great novelist Thomas Hardy, hers was a kind of open house for cats. Hardy, once asked about all the cats clustered by the tea table, explained that only some of them were his: 'Some are cats who come regularly to have tea, and some are still other cats, not invited by us, but who seem to find about this time of day that tea will be going.'

Gaynor's visitors included a pair of local fluffy cats, obviously well cared for, who regularly spent time in her garden and occasionally snacked on the hedgehog food. Then there was Sam, a local cat who came in during the day to relax in her company when his owners were out. Almost every day he turned up in the morning, pushed in through the cat flap, and spent his time sleeping peacefully on her sofa. He needed somewhere warm during the daytime because the central heating in his own house was turned off while everybody was out at work. He, too, expected, and received, a little snack.

'Sometimes the local hedgehogs don't get a look in when it comes to their food,' Gaynor admitted. Sam used to bring his mother with him to Gaynor's house, until one day she stopped accompanying him and Gaynor never knew why.

As most cat lovers know, some cats, like Sam, two-time their official owners. Like faithless human partners, cats often set up two families, and thus two dinners. Charlie, who lived in a village near me, pulled off the three-owner, three-dinner trick. He had his official owner, one unofficial owner and a house where he spent much of his time during the day. I discovered this while knocking on doors looking for my own missing black cat. 'Charlie is our cat,' said the people working in one of the gardens. 'I've adopted Charlie,' said the woman two doors along. 'I'm not Charlie's owner,' admitted the householder three doors on, 'but he spends most of his day with me.' I kept Charlie's secret and didn't let on to the other two what he was up to.

Percy, Gaynor's elderly cat, was an example of how a cat will rehome himself if he feels like it, or if his original home is not up to scratch by feline standards. Neglected or abused dogs may stick around and suffer. Cats move out. Percy, indeed, had done this. His human 'parents' had divorced 15 years earlier and he had been left with the man, who, to Percy's disgust, had bought a dog. Percy had promptly rehomed himself with Gaynor. 'He started coming in at night, then started staying during the day, too,' she explained.

The new ginger visitor didn't look like a cat who already had an owner, though; or even a cat who had left an unsatisfactory home. He looked like a homeless down and out, a street cat who was struggling, and failing, to survive.

He certainly needed help urgently. It was November, not a good month for any cat to be living on the streets. The leaves had fallen off the trees and the English weather had settled into being cold and wet. 'He looked desperate,' Gaynor remembered.

I knew Gaynor from her work as Gaynor the Trainer.

11

She would arrive at my house once a week in a 4x4 car full of weights, mats, huge rubber balls and other training equipment. At the time the ginger cat turned up in her garden, I was caring for my husband, Ronnie, who was suffering from prostate cancer, bone cancer and lung cancer.

Ronnie was – and still is – the love of my life. When I first met him, he was a war reporter and diplomatic correspondent. But it was his early years, before I was even born, that were the secret of his attraction. They say dogs and women follow marching men. Ronnie had been a Royal Marine Commando in the Second World War and, to me, he was still the marine he had once been. Once a marine, always a marine – at least in my heart. A big bear of a man, he enveloped me in his hugs.

But now he could hug no more. The man I loved was slowly leaving me. He was disabled not just by the cancer but from a helicopter accident he'd survived while reporting on a small war in Oman in the 1970s. It had broken his back, although he recovered and lived without pain for the next 30 years. Then in his old age, the pain of that helicopter crash settled into his spine, wreaking havoc with the nerves of his lower back.

Now he lived with pain every single day, never complaining but slowly getting worse as the cancer weakened his body. His spirit was still strong. He was confined to an armchair in the living room for much of the day, just able to walk from room to room but unable to manage stairs. Once a week, I would work out in the living room while he looked on, which is where Gaynor the Trainer, as she calls herself, came into our lives, and through her, the ginger cat.

At the time I first contacted her it was about exercise not

cats. I was recovering from a mastectomy for breast cancer. We were a double-cancer household and it was difficult for me to leave Ronnie alone without somebody sitting in the house to look after him. Gaynor ran exercise and Pilates classes, as well as a bespoke cake-making business. As I could not get to her classes, she came to me.

Gaynor isn't one of those young, slim personal trainers with perfect bodies who make you feel old and ugly and unfit as soon as you set eyes on them. Nor was she one of those personal trainers who set themselves up without any special expertise. She specialized in complex needs and the kind of client whom safety-conscious gymnasiums sometimes refuse to help. At the point we met I fell into the special needs category.

Being younger than Ronnie, I wasn't in such bad shape as he was but I wasn't very well. The comfort of Gaynor was that she understood how difficult exercise can be after an operation. She had suffered at the hands of the National Health Service when a knee operation went very wrong, leaving her in constant pain and requiring two further major operations. Despite this, she had rehabilitated herself back to fitness.

So she used to visit weekly to give me a work-out, focusing mainly on restoring my right arm to its normal function. I was missing a bit of underarm muscle, which had been taken out at the same time the breast was taken away. If the muscle is left, it makes a brick-like bulge under the arm. Taken away, it can knit itself back – more or less.

Thanks to Gaynor's exercises I was regaining strength in the affected arm, although I was still finding it slightly painful to stretch up to get something from a very high shelf.

'Owww...' I was puffing and panting my way through

a work-out with weights, pushing them up, then forward, then down.

'You're exercising your pecs and lats. Most of all, it's the pectoral major muscle over the breast you need to strengthen.' Gaynor believes in explaining the exact benefits of what her clients are doing. My right pectoral muscle needed all the exercise it could get so that my right arm could move as freely as my left. My aim was to strengthen it so that I could lift weights with my right as well as left arm.

'Now to the exercise I showed you last week. By the way, do you want another cat? A stray has turned up in my garden.' Gaynor's exercises were always accompanied by encouraging explanations and cat talk. I loved the cat talk. Any thought of cats lifts my spirits. She was nearly as obsessed with cats as I am.

'Well …' puff, puff '… I have been thinking I have space for one more. But it's got to be a small cat who can't bully Tilly.' Tilly often spent her morning indolently lying in the living room watching me exercise. Not that she joined in. My exertions seemed to amuse her. She enjoyed the superiority of looking down on me from the armchair when I was lying on the exercise mat.

While Ronnie was heart of my heart, Tilly ran him a pretty close second. I had taken her in as a foster cat after she had languished for 18 months in a cat pen, unable to find a home. She was small, grey-brown and, when I first got her, utterly terrified. On arrival she had lived under the bed for almost three months, too frightened to come out. The idea was that I would rehabilitate her so that she could find a home as a house pet. By the time she had become confident enough to be calm and loving, I had grown to love her so much I couldn't hand her on. From being her fosterer I had become her owner.

When Gaynor mentioned the possibility of another cat, Ronnie intervened. He was being loving enough not to laugh at my efforts, although occasionally his lips would twitch with amusement.

'I want a kitten,' he said. 'Or at least a pretty cat this time.'

If Tilly had been able to understand human language, she would not have been pleased. In my eyes, she was beautiful but, it must be admitted, nobody else had thought enough of her to adopt her during the 18 months she languished unchosen in a Cats Protection cat pen.

'The stray is a lovely ginger colour,' Gaynor said, hopefully.

This sounded promising. Ronnie, who came to love cats late in life, had been seduced into that love by their beauty. His favourite had been William, an elegant, semi-long-haired tabby and white, whom he had picked out of a basket of kittens. William was everything Ronnie felt a cat should be – stunningly handsome, graceful and dignified. Tilly, who was ugly, not very graceful and not at all dignified, didn't fit the template. He didn't want another Tilly.

She was not looking her best that morning anyway. She had been mousing in the nearby dry barn but had had to make her way home through the rain. When she was wet, her soft brown fur stuck together and looked unkempt despite her daily careful grooming. She looked a mess.

She is a very small cat, not much larger than a Singapura, one of the smallest pedigree breeds. Her semi-long, soft hair makes her look dumpy and short-legged. In a good light, if the sun is shining through her brown and grey soft hair, highlighting some ginger streaks in it, she can look as beautiful as ever William was – at least, in my eyes.

'That's very good. You couldn't have done that a month ago,' said Gaynor as I worked on the weights. Her speciality, other than cats and making cakes, is encouragement – lavish encouragement for the slightest kind of effort; enough encouragement to make even a reluctant exerciser (which I was) want to see her again.

'Would you like to see his photo?' she asked, switching from exercise to cats. This was a move of low cunning on her part, motivated by her natural desire to find Toby a good home. Cat photos are addictive for cat lovers. The millions of cat photos, videos, blogs and websites on the internet prove that!

She showed the photo first to Ronnie for his approval. She knew I was a soft touch anyway and it was Ronnie who needed persuading. On the small, mobile-phone screen, Toby looked surprisingly handsome. Painfully thin top models often look good in photos and so did he!

Ronnie responded well. He was attracted by the blotchy ginger markings down Toby's body, the fluffy tail and the strong whiskers. Either side of Toby's cheeks longer fur merged into his ruff.

'He looks like Damian Lewis with sideburns,' said Ronnie, who had been watching the TV thriller series *Homeland*. He did, too – in fact, he was better looking, I thought.

'He looks like Orlando the Marmalade Cat to me,' I said. I had been brought up on children's stories in which the animals had been heroes, including *Little Grey Rabbit*, *Black Beauty*, *Said the Cat to the Dog*, *Puss in Boots* and, of course, *Orlando the Marmalade Cat* with its many sequels. *Orlando the Marmalade*

Cat was one of my favourites. Still is.

Toby had the same ginger markings. He had Orlando's white chin, white whiskers and even the same white tufts of hair growing out of his ears. His sideburns, however, were longer than Orlando's and it looked as if his hair might be a little more fluffy. Moreover, Toby, like Orlando, had 'eyes like gooseberries', the green of under-ripe gooseberries, the sort you have to cook rather than eat raw. There was one small difference, which I did not notice at the time of looking at the photo. Toby was cross-eyed.

Each of his gooseberry green eyes had a pupil that slanted inwards. In that first photo, the eyes were only slightly crossed. Later, I discovered that this squint, with the absurd scientific name of convergent strabismus, came and went. At times it was very pronounced indeed, and if he had been human, he would have needed spectacles.

Gaynor did *not* draw attention to his faulty eyes. Instead, she pointed out, 'He's very small. He's hardly bigger than Tilly.' Now this was an even cleverer remark. She knew that I would worry about small Tilly's safety and happiness with a big cat. I'd already mentioned it.

'That sounds good,' I said. 'If he's full grown, that's safer than getting a kitten. A kitten might grow to be too large.' This remark, it turned out, was completely wrong. But I was half won over.

'I'd take him on myself,' said Gaynor, 'but it wouldn't be fair on Percy. He's too old. Percy's been wonderful to the two kittens and Indie absolutely adores him. But I think another adult male might be too much competition for him.' In this, Gaynor's judgment was better than mine, but, as I have admitted, I was already weakening. Even in the mobile-phone photo, you could see that the ginger cat was thin and his coat was scruffy. He had what seemed like a handsome fluffy tail and nice facial whiskers, but the rest of his fur coat looked awful.

'I don't think he'll survive the winter,' said Gaynor, hopefully. She hasn't been a personal trainer for years without knowing how to motivate people. Lavish encouragement was, as I've said, her *forte*. She knew how to get into my head and switch on the 'just one more cat' syndrome – not that it's very difficult.

'It's getting colder,' said Gaynor, ramping up the motivation. 'I think he may be sleeping under the car or perhaps under the bushes in the front of the house. He's so pathetic.' Of course, I knew and she knew that if I didn't take Toby, she would rescue him anyway. But this expert in motivating others had succeeded in making me feel I must do something.

'Why don't I take him in and see how it goes. At least I can give him somewhere to live for the time being.'

Normally, I would just have arranged for him to be picked up by my local cat rescue, but I knew that they might not be able to afford to do so. Sunshine Cat Rescue had started up as a small charity and they were horribly short of funds. This cat might be the one that broke their bank balance. But the thought of him living in the shrubs or under Gaynor's car was really upsetting. While a car might keep off the relentless November rain from above, it could not keep off the rain that would pool in the gravel drive. Cats hate getting their feet wet. This cat was having to live and sleep with permanently wet feet.

Yes, I had room in my house. Yes, I had the money to pay his veterinary bills (although these were to be much larger than

I'd thought). As I could barely leave home during this period, I wasn't doing much shopping. I went out when I knew exactly what I wanted and could bowl into the shop, buy it and rush back home. So I wasn't spending money on casual luxuries. I could afford to nurse Toby back to health. For me, having another cat, even one that I would rehome, *was* a luxury, and one that I could afford.

More important than either of these considerations was the fact that I just couldn't walk by on the other side and leave this pathetic stray to his fate. From Gaynor's account, it seemed that he might not last much longer on the streets. Shelter from the wet and cold is as important to a cat's survival as regular food. Even with regular meals from her hedgehog bowl, he might well not make it through the winter. (At this point cat lovers will realize that my judgment was clouded by my desire for another cat. Gaynor would never have left him to starve!)

Yet how would Tilly feel if I added a new cat to the household? She had started life in the garden of a cat hoarder – one of several cats who lived in an open-sided shed with only dustbins laid on their sides for shelter. Then during her 18 months in a cat pen, waiting for the adoption that never came, she had obviously loathed the companion cat who shared the pen with her. I couldn't pretend that she would be delighted with a companion. She and I were so close that another cat might interfere with our relationship.

Tilly was special to me because I'd had to earn her trust over months. When she first came to live with me, she had lived under the bed in the spare bedroom, coming out only at night. Even then, every time I moved towards her she would run away; and the only way I could stop her was to run away myself! That way she didn't have to run, because I did it for her, so to speak.

The more work I put into trying to tame Tilly, the more I fell in love with her. As the Fox in the story of *The Little Prince* says: 'People have forgotten this truth ... You become responsible forever for what you've tamed.'

Most people realize that if we love somebody, we will make an effort to care for them in practical terms. What they forget is that if we do caring actions for somebody even before we love them, we begin to love them, and our own efforts (not theirs) will make us love more deeply. The object of our care becomes the object of our love. This deepening love has been, I believe, the inner journey in every relationship I have had with all my cats. They have taught me as much as I have taught them.

My taming of Tilly had taught me this love. I had felt huge delight as she began to blossom into a much-loved pet. I had seen her change from a scruffy, frightened cat who did not even look after her own fur into a relaxed and happy cat who spent a lot of her time grooming herself.

I had seen her learn how to go outdoors and hunt, and I had seen her begin to play. When she had first come to me, I had sometimes heard her at dead of night playing with a piece of old newspaper. Slowly, as she grew more confident, she began to play in sight of me. She would bat a catnip mouse, pull my spectacles off the bedside table, pull at the cord of the bathroom blind or chase my fishing-rod toy.

Moreover, as she recovered she taught me an even more valuable lesson. As Ronnie had grown both weaker and more disabled, and as I recovered from my own breast cancer, I realized I needed to imitate Tilly. She had regained her ability to look after herself as she became less frightened. Her grooming was exemplary. Copying her example, I made a real effort to look after myself. I went for long walks in the open air, either alone or with my local archaeology club, whenever I could safely leave Ronnie. This put pleasure and play into my life, just as Tilly had shown me.

Even so, looking after Ronnie was stressful. I lived with daily anxiety about what might happen next. Once I had arrived home after a walk to find him flat on the floor below the stairs. He had fallen off the stair lift. Luckily, there was no blood and he was fully conscious. I decided to try to get him up by myself. I propped him up using various cushions from the back of the armchairs and sofa but found I could not do it on my own. I phoned round friends until I found someone who could help me. Somehow we managed without calling for an ambulance.

For some people, adding a starving, ill cat to an invalid's household would have just added a new stress to an already stressful situation. This was not the case for me. My ways of dealing with stress were limited. I had given up alcohol so I couldn't turn to drink. I was already somewhat overweight so overeating was not an option. A new cat was just what I needed. Cats reduce rather than increase my stress. A new feline worry would distract my mind from the continual, more serious anxieties about Ronnie.

'Do you think Tilly could cope with another cat?' I asked Gaynor. 'What is he like with your cats?'

'He rolls in front of them,' she said. 'He never attacks them. There have been no fights. Indie and Lily are fine with him. It's just Percy I'm worried about, because of his age. You'll see. He's a very gentle cat. Tilly will be fine.'

At heart, I knew that Tilly would prefer to be on her own in the house. Cats can cope with companions, but living with another cat isn't natural for them. Cats often live very happily with their relatives, the cats they have known from kittenhood, but many of them don't do real friendship with unrelated cats.

I told myself that Tilly had been brought up in a cat hoarder's household so would be OK eventually with this cat's companionship. I'd taken in foster cats twice previously. Both had come to stay in the spare room in an emergency, and she had shown interest in them rather than either disgust or fear. With elderly James, a ginger cat with severe health difficulties, she had been cautious but fascinated. I had come to the conclusion that he had just a little time left to live, so I had let him out of the spare room into the household. He was very affectionate and enjoyed human contact. He just ignored Tilly, which seemed to reassure her. She had also nipped into the spare room when I was looking after another elderly ill cat, Chester, over the Christmas period. Chester had hissed, so she had retreated, but she didn't seem too worried about it. She was still bold enough to try to steal his food. Both foster cats had been male. I hoped she would cope with this third male cat.

I turned to Ronnie. 'How do you feel about it?' I asked him. 'We could call him Gussie Fink-Nottle like the character in the Jeeves stories.' I am a big fan of Wodehouse.

'Not that,' said Ronnie. He wasn't arguing about another cat, just about the name. 'I hate that name.'

'What about Bingo Little, then? He's a small cat.'

'No, we'll call him Toby,' Ronnie said firmly.

Ronnie had named him, and by naming him, he had accepted Toby into his life, the life of a strong man being weakened, the life that he and I knew was at the beginning of the end.

'Why Toby?' I asked. 'It's a dog's name.'

'*Twelfth Night*. Look it up,' he replied, smiling.

I did. Sir Toby Belch is a comic character in Shakespeare's *Twelfth Night,* fond of drinking, singing and having fun. There wasn't much fun in Ronnie's life, which was why he chose the name. Perhaps a small, ginger, furry companion could add a little light relief. If things worked out, this new cat would, I decided, be *his* cat rather than mine. Ronnie *needed* a cat.

The ginger cat's small size was the final deciding factor. He was too small to intimidate Tilly. Besides, I told myself that if he and Tilly didn't get on, I would simply pay for whatever vet's treatment he needed and pass him on to my local cat rescue.

'I'll see how it goes,' I said to Gaynor and Ronnie. 'I can always find him a new home if he and Tilly don't get on.'

As it turned out, this prediction was famously wrong.

Chapter 2

If you love someone, you clean up their poo

'Celia, I've got him. He's in my office. Do you want to come and fetch him?'

The decision had been made. Ronnie had acquiesced in that decision. Now Gaynor was making sure it happened. We had agreed that I would take him on and rehome him if he didn't settle down well with Tilly. More importantly, I would make sure that he didn't have to go on living under the cars on the estate. It was November, it was very wet and Gaynor didn't think he would survive much longer. He needed rescuing without delay.

What she hadn't actually told me was that she was going to pick him up and take him in later that same day. She wasn't going to give me time to have second thoughts, so she phoned me the following morning.

Gaynor lives about ten minutes away from me, so I could fetch the stray cat immediately. I usually could not leave Ronnie alone for very long in the mornings. He was on medication that meant he had to pee frequently, and that meant I had to be around to help him. Mornings, about an hour after he had taken the pill, were the worst times.

I had considered moving the medication to the evening but that would simply have meant getting up at hourly intervals throughout the night. As it was, I was already getting up four or five times a night. Moving the medication would probably have meant waking up to help him even more frequently, probably about seven times a night. So I opted for morning toilet attendance duties rather than more of a nighttime vigil.

I grabbed the cat carrier – the sort with a solid bottom in case a terrified cat lost control of its bowels – put in a towel just in case the new cat panicked in this way during the journey, and drove over to Gaynor's. Toby had allowed Gaynor to pick him up the previous evening, so obviously he was domesticated, not feral, but he might never have been in a car before and once cat pee or poo gets into a car seat, even steam cleaning doesn't entirely clear up the smell. When it comes to selling the car, the value is naturally somewhat lower than it might have been. In such minor ways do cats affect our lives!

'He used the litter tray during the night,' Gaynor announced. 'I think I can just pick him up and put him in the carrier.' And so she did.

As she brought him out of her office and into the living room, where I had the carrier, her own cats looked on with interest. Elderly Percy on his windowsill seemed relaxed about the situation. After all, the intruder into the garden was now

26

being taken away. Indie and Lily, the two younger cats, looked a little more uncertain, perhaps being cautious not just about Toby but about my presence. They were rescue feral kittens and had missed some of the vital first contact with humans. So it had taken them a long time fully to relax in the presence of people other than Gaynor and her mother.

I was a bit dismayed by what I saw. I was expecting him to look scrawny and ragged. What I wasn't expecting was his look of utter defeat. His body wasn't tense with fear, nor was it relaxed and happy. He sagged in Gaynor's arms in helpless surrender to whatever was going to happen to him next. He looked as if he was too ill to care about anything much. Here was a cat that had nearly given up the struggle to survive.

As I drove Toby home, I wondered if this rescue had been such a good idea. Now, as well as day and night caring for a very ill husband, I had to care for a traumatized cat. Then I remembered how fulfilling it would be to have an extra cat. I don't approve of too many cats in a house, and I certainly didn't want to turn into a mad cat hoarder. But just one more, making a total of two, should be OK. If Toby imitated his namesake, he would bring some fun into our lives.

My plan was to install him in the main bedroom. I no longer slept there. I'd moved onto the sofa in the living room so as to be close to Ronnie at night. If Toby was as tame as Gaynor suggested, he would probably want to hide in the cardboard box I had put in there for him.

It was an ordinary cardboard wine box, covered at the top, with a fleece inside and an entrance hole cut into the side. An ideal place, I thought, for the first few hours in his new home. Other foster cats had hidden under the beds in the spare

27

bedroom but our large double bed – alas, no longer the haven and heaven for Ronnie and me – went all the way down to the floor. There was no space for frightened cats underneath.

I had put out two litter trays full of small grain litter, just in case he was one of those cats who wanted one for pee and one for poo. Hadn't Gaynor told me that he had used the litter tray in her office? That was promising. The trays were carefully sited in two locations – one in the small bathroom, just outside the shower, and one in the bedroom as far as possible from the food area. I had put the food bowl on a tea tray, so that if he was a messy eater, bits would not fall on the carpet. The water bowl, also carefully sited away from the food bowl, was placed directly on the carpet. If some water got spilled, that wouldn't matter. It wouldn't leave a stain like food would.

Oh yes, I had planned it all out beautifully.

Part of the plan was to keep the new cat in quarantine. When he had settled in (just a day or two, I hoped) I would get him cleaned up to get rid of fleas, ear mites and worms, tested for FIV and microchipped. He needed to be kept away from Tilly until this was all done. In particular, the FIV test was vital.

If he was FIV positive, his future would be uncertain. I would not put Tilly's health at risk. It's true that the FIV virus can be spread only in saliva and blood, so that she would be unlikely to catch it unless they had a fight. But what if they did fight? At this point I couldn't know how or whether they would get on.

And if he *was* FIV positive, would my local cat rescue take him on? I wasn't sure. As a small, independent charity then chronically short of money, they might not have been in a position to do so. Finding a home for an FIV positive cat usually takes some time because the home has to be indoor only. These are common in big cities, less common in rural areas like mine. Most people in the UK want to give their cats the chance to roam and have feline fun out of doors.

Toby also needed one other veterinary intervention. He still had his manhood (or should it be tomhood?). No doubt he had sired some beautiful ginger kittens on the estate where he lived, but that had to stop. I wouldn't keep a smelly tomcat in my home. Luckily, he didn't know what I had planned. Neither did Ronnie at this stage. Ronnie had always been rather sensitive about this aspect of tomcat ownership.

When I arrived home with the cat carrier, the podiatrist was attending to Ronnie's feet. I briefly showed him Toby in the carrier and went upstairs.

'He's a nice colour,' said Ronnie. He sounded positive.

Upstairs, I put down the cat carrier on the floor of the bedroom, opened it and the new cat staggered out, looking bewildered. I couldn't stay to see any more. I had to go down to watch how the podiatrist dressed one of Ronnie's toes, which he had somehow injured, perhaps by bumping it against his walking frame.

'Celia, you will have to change the bandage in ten days' time, so watch what I'm doing,' she instructed.

When she left, I went back upstairs to see the new cat. He had completely disappeared. He couldn't have taken refuge under the bed because there was no room there. I looked under the chest of drawers in case he had squeezed himself into that narrow space, but there was no sign of him. 'Somehow, he has got out,' I thought, but all the windows were closed.

Then I had a thought. I couldn't see him anywhere

but perhaps Tilly could find him, like a sniffer dog finds an explosive. By now, she was hovering outside the bedroom door, full of curiosity. I let her in and she went straight to the wardrobe. Right in the far corner of it was Toby. He had hidden himself behind a long dress, amid several pairs of shoes. I hurriedly took Tilly out of the room, now she had detected him. He was meant to be in quarantine so she could not be allowed to make physical contact. Then I took a look at the cat who was to be her companion.

Hunched among the shoes, half hidden by my dresses, filthy and terrified, he looked as if he might be seriously ill. He was toastrack thin, with all his ribs sticking out. I could see the ribs even through his longish hair. The fur itself was clotted with dirt and engine oil, so that after touching him I would need to wash my hands. I could see clumps of hair that were sticking together. His only relatively clean areas were his paws, his bushy tail and his wide sideburns. These reminded me of Beatrix Potter's *Tale of Mr Tod,* the story of a gingery fox with similar sideburns. They gave him a rather raffish look. Ronnie was right. There was something of Toby Belch about this cat!

He was small, only about an inch or two at the shoulder bigger than Tilly, and Tilly was a very small cat. His whiskers were white, disappointingly short, and there was a little white irregular patch at the end of his tail. His chin had little black bits on it – I thought these were just dirt. His ears were filthy with black smears on the hairs that came out of the ear holes.

All in all, this cat looked in a really bad way. I wondered whether he was near to dying of starvation, or maybe his thin body was a symptom of cancer. It might be the FIV virus was kicking in and wrecking his immune system.

I'd give him a chance, I decided. If he tested FIV positive, with this degree of emaciation it meant the virus had progressed quite far. It would probably be kinder to put him down. I would ask for the vet's opinion. If he was clear of FIV, on the other hand, the emaciation was just lack of food. Once he was cleaned up and castrated he would definitely find a home. Ginger cats are popular.

'Or I might keep him if he is kind to Ronnie,' I thought. There should be something in Ronnie's life that was funny and carefree. Toby wouldn't think less of Ronnie because he was old and ill, and Ronnie would think better of Toby because he was – or would be once he had scrubbed up – good-looking.

Tilly could never be a substitute for William, the beautiful tabby and white and Ronnie's favourite. She was not beautiful in Ronnie's eyes and, worse still, she was still rather a one-woman (me) cat. When she came to live with me, Ronnie was already ill, and this had made it more difficult for her to bond closely with him. He could no longer safely bend down to stroke her and she was worried by the fact he walked first with a stick, then with a walking frame.

'I don't really want another Tilly,' he had said firmly to me. He could be forgiven for not finding Tilly very amusing. She was frightened of his high hospital bed and wouldn't jump up on it; nor was she happy at getting up on his lap on the special hospital chair. So he didn't get a lot of affection from her. She saved her kindnesses for me.

About four years before the arrival of Toby, Ronnie had been diagnosed with advanced prostate cancer that had spread into the bone. 'The average lifespan is two years, after a diagnosis of advanced prostate cancer,' the young doctor in the cancer clinic had told him. Well, he *had* asked. I had watched Ronnie's face. It went white with shock.

Worse was to come that day. We were sent off to the cancer nurse, a lovely, kind woman. 'Do the things you want to do but haven't got round to doing,' she said helpfully. It was not a very cheerful thought, however.

The next day his GP said, much more helpfully, 'More people die with prostate cancer than die of it.' Comforting words, and for a man in his eighties likely to be true. Cancer is a disease of the elderly but the older you are, the slower it goes. He was put on medication and by the time Toby arrived in our lives, he had beaten the average by two years and had lived double the forecast time.

A year before Toby arrived, Ronnie had also been diagnosed with lung cancer – hardly surprising after a near lifetime of pipe smoking. This time, wiser than the first time, he had not asked about the prognosis. I hope he didn't realize how short it was likely to be. Alas, I knew.

Ronnie had always been a big man, several inches over six foot, wide at the shoulder and the waist, overweight but not obese. As a doctor had said when he was in his prime, 'Ronnie, you are fat but fit.' As a foreign correspondent and war reporter he had covered almost every Middle Eastern and North African war since about the mid-1950s, calling a halt after the 1990 Gulf War. At the age of 64, he became too old to insure at a sensible cost, so his foreign adventures had to stop.

His large frame with its cuddly avoirdupois, and a cracked spine after the helicopter accident in Oman, had not prevented him from going to wars. I was used to coming home to find his battered old typewriter gone and a scribbled and often illegible note saying something like, 'Off to Turkish invasion of Cyprus.' Like an old warhorse exulting in his strength and going out to meet the battle, Ronnie would get his things together and disappear, often before I had even realized war had broken out in that particular country.

Now this big bear of a man was half the size. The broken spine from the helicopter accident had taken three inches off his height so he was no longer taller than I was, but almost the same height. Cancer seemed to have taken off a further two inches so he was now becoming shorter than me. It had also devoured about five stone off his frame. As he had joked to a shocked cancer nurse at the hospital: 'Fight the Flab. To Lose Weight, Get Cancer.' By the time Toby arrived at our house, it was difficult to tell which of the two was the most emaciated.

Maybe Toby could do for Ronnie what Tilly could not. If nothing else, Toby was – or would be when recovered – better looking than she was. And Ronnie had fallen in love with William, Tilly's predecessor, partly because William was a beautiful long-haired tabby and white with deep golden eyes outlined in black. Toby didn't look as if he would become as beautiful as William – few cats could be – but there was no doubt that, when healthy, Toby would be very handsome. Ronnie would like seeing a good-looking cat around the house.

With luck, Toby might also be more likely than Tilly to give Ronnie some much-needed affection. On the day of Toby's arrival, it was too soon for the two to bond. Ronnie couldn't even come to see this cat cowering in the wardrobe, for he was too ill by now to get upstairs even with the stair lift.

'I can't even take a look at him,' he complained.

'He'll come out,' I reassured him. 'Gaynor says he let

himself be picked up so he is obviously less frightened of humans than Tilly was. He will be out exploring the house in days not weeks.'

This turned out to be rather an optimistic forecast. Toby would not come out at all. He cowered there, his body pressed against the back wall of the wardrobe. During the first two days he emerged from his hiding place to eat, but only when I was not in the room. And, boy, did he eat. He ate voraciously, at least four envelopes of cat food a day, and after each envelope, the bowl had been licked clean.

Food was the way to his heart. On day three he came out of his wardrobe when I put cat biscuits within his view and stepped back far enough. He was so run down, so painfully weak, that as I gently stroked his back, tufts of hair fell on to the floor.

His back legs looked slightly odd and he seemed to walk with an odd gait. Indeed, apart from his tail, his whole back end appeared rather fragile. At first I thought that perhaps this was just the body shape of an uncastrated tomcat. They often have a front half that is thicker and heavier than the back half. Then I wondered if it might be something more serious.

Toby's huge food intake meant an equally huge output! Worse still, he had chronic diarrhoea. This was very bad news indeed, since Toby did not use the litter trays. He was happy to use them for pee but not for poo.

At first he merely defecated on the bathroom rug that was near one of the litter trays. So I cut a small piece of the soiled area out of the rug, and put it in a third litter tray. The idea was that he would continue the use the rug, only this time it would be in the tray. And that would help him get used to the idea of doing it in the tray. Alas, he did nothing of the kind.

The next time he decided to dump on the bathroom floor. That wasn't too bad, so I was encouraged to believe that things might get easier. I didn't have any spare pieces of vinyl flooring to put into the litter tray and I could hardly gouge some out of the bathroom floor. On the other hand, if he decided to use vinyl reliably, it was, at least, easy to clean.

However, he used the vinyl just once. Next, he christened the bed itself. He left a large pile of excrement on the duvet and also decided to relieve himself of urine there. When cats pee or poo on the bed, it may be a sign that they are, drastically, scent marking where they can smell loved owners. This interpretation seemed overly optimistic to me.

On the third day, just for a change, he backed up against the trouser press and defecated there from standing height.

His behaviour ran counter to cat-behaviour theory. The theory is plain. Cats get used to a certain substance under their feet when it comes to toileting and will reliably defecate on the same type of substance. Toby, indeed, proved this to be true as far as pee was concerned. Apart from the one time when he relieved himself on the duvet, he always urinated in the litter trays. So far so good.

But when it came to the excrement, he seemed to be without preferences. So far there had been the rug, the bathroom floor, the duvet and now the vertical trouser press – four completely different surfaces.

The following day he experimented with the bedroom carpet near the wardrobe. And the day after he picked on an area of carpet near the little bookcase. So much for cats having reliable preferences!

Down on my hands and knees I rubbed resentfully at the carpet. I wore rubber gloves to clean up, just as I had on the previous days. My right arm has missing lymph nodes, major sites for immune cells. The nodes were taken out when my right breast was removed, so I have to be careful when it comes to unpleasant body fluids, whether feline or human, getting on the right hand and arm.

I was used to clearing up poo. Cleaning up Ronnie's poo had at first seemed worse than cleaning up used cat litter, which has the advantage of the poo being covered with small pieces. I had never minded cleaning the litter tray and would usually do it twice or three times a day. Cleaning up Ronnie was worse to begin with, much worse. I had to fight against dry heaves. Then over the weeks I got used to it and could clean him up as easily as I could a litter tray.

Alas, Toby's poo was not in a litter tray and the nature of it suggested he might have some kind of stomach bug. The four envelopes of cat food were seemingly difficult for him to digest. Perhaps months of eating out of dustbins had shot his digestive system to hell. I wondered if the digestive problems were a sign of hyperthyroidism, a common complaint in middle-aged to elderly cats. Perhaps the emaciated ribs were a sign of illness as well as starvation.

Like Ronnie, Toby couldn't help making a mess, but I didn't love him as much as I did Ronnie. I loved Ronnie, so I was willing to clean up his poo occasionally. I had to do it, if I was to keep him in his own home, rather than thrust him into an old people's nursing home.

But what was I going to do about Toby? At this point my feelings towards him were rapidly cooling from lukewarm to cold. I hadn't known him long enough to feel any love. I felt only pity. Cowering in the wardrobe, he wasn't inviting or offering any affection. His erratic toilet habits were distinctly worrying. The bedroom was beginning to smell. I had had to wash the duvet and now I was scrubbing the carpet or vinyl daily.

I was worried, too, about hygiene. Ronnie was now so ill that his immune system was very weak indeed. Mine was much, much better, except for the hand and arm I used for scrubbing.

One solution to the difficulty was to keep Toby in a lavatory, with vinyl and no carpet on the floor. As long as I always wore rubber gloves, cleaning up would not be a threat to me. But the tiny *en suite* lavatory and shower next to my bedroom was too small to fit in two litter trays (one for pee and one for poo), a food tray, a water bowl and a cat bed.

I did, however, have another larger bathroom that would have been suitable. It had twice the space. It would have allowed me time to get him properly litter trained, without too much clearing up. Bathroom floors are easy to clean, unlike carpet or trouser presses.

This bathroom, however, was booked. I needed it for the live-in carer. A carer came one week in four to give me a chance to get out and about. The latest was going to arrive in three days' time. I could hardly expect *her* to share a bathroom with a cat that used the floor as a toilet.

Tilly had been the inspiration for my getting more help. I could not let Toby compromise that. Tilly had slowly changed, from a miserable, ugly little cat who didn't even bother to keep her fur clean, into a splendidly fluffy, clean little feline. She had shown me that self-care was the essence of being healthy and (if possible) happy. It was her influence that had helped me make more effort to look after myself. I shouldn't just cancel the live-in carer for the sake of a stray cat.

At this stage, Tilly was intrigued rather than upset by the new visitor. Keeping to my quarantine rule, I didn't let her have any direct contact with Toby. He probably had every common parasite, outer and inner, he might turn out to be FIV positive and the litter-tray troubles suggested other possible infections. He was a walking collection of possible health problems.

I reckoned I had got him just in time, before the winter killed him off, but it was looking as if he might not be the ideal guest in our house. I considered putting him in the garden shed with a cat bed, but by now it was too cold at night. Even with proper food, he might not survive in a shed.

'Why not put him in a cattery for a little while?' my cat-mad nephew suggested, and that made me think of Julie, who runs the local Finstock Cattery. Unlike some cattery owners, she will board cats with diabetes, cats on special diets and cats that need regular medication or even regular injections. She is also wise in the way of rescue cats. She has taken in, cared for and helped scores of homeless felines. What is more, she is brilliant at finding them homes. People who have used her cattery regularly often go to her if they want a new cat, and she always has one.

Her most spectacular successful turnaround was when she took in two homeless British Blues, Caesar and Cleo, a brother and sister. They came in one Friday afternoon and she put a photo of them on the rescue website. They were adopted and taken to a new home the following day.

The secret of her rehoming success is that she tells all her customers about the cats that need a home, and then asks them to tell all their friends, and *their* friends to tell *their* friends. The news of a cat needing a home travels from mouth to mouth until a home is found, rather like non-digital Facebook sharing.

Naturally, Julie's own cats are all rescues. Gym was picked up near the local gymnasium and brought back from the USA. Garfield looked just like Garfield. Thai, a white kitten with a taste for porridge, had been living on scraps in the village, and then there was Tripps, a black cat with a white smudge on his nose whose family had given him up.

Oh yes, and at the time of Toby's arrival she also had a rescue German Shepherd, now settling down nicely after having been handed nine times from home to new home. In the past, she had also raised a fledgling bird, which had to be fed every half an hour through the day and night. So a stray ginger cat with bad toilet habits was nothing much to her.

But first I had to take Toby to the vet. To do this, I had to pick him up and put him in the carrier. How would he respond?

So far I hadn't touched him. If I put a trail of cat biscuits, he would tentatively come out of his wardrobe for a few feet to eat them, tolerating my presence in the room and allowing a sly stroke. But having eaten the biscuits, he would scuttle back to his hiding place. Most of his out-of-wardrobe excursions, whether to eat, use the litter tray or to defecate in a new place, had taken place when I was absent.

I got the cat carrier ready, with a piece of fleece on the bottom of it, and took it into the bedroom, placing it, open, on the bed. Then I strode towards the wardrobe, knelt down and masterfully scooped up Toby. He didn't struggle. He didn't scratch. He didn't bite. He just stiffened a little, then sagged.

Getting him into the cat carrier was a little more difficult, but I pushed him in and closed the door on him.

It was then that he struggled. He threw himself against the door several times, then burrowed under the fleece in a miserable heap. He stayed immobile under the fleece throughout the journey to the vet's surgery.

On the vet's table, he was still motionless with terror but accepted the vet's handling without biting. William always used to bite the vet, turning round for a particularly strong nip when the thermometer was up his backside. Poor Toby stayed frozen with fear through this indignity.

The good news was that he was so young that hyperthyroidism could be ruled out. The vet thought he was thin because of worms. It seemed unlikely that he was FIV positive but he was tested just in case. Most FIV positive cats have fight wounds, where the virus has gained entry to the body. Toby was not neutered but he didn't have the scarred ears and face of a veteran tomcat fighter.

'I'm afraid he can't be neutered till he has recovered a little. He's not well enough for an anaesthetic,' said the vet. So Toby was wormed, de-flead and given the first vaccination. It cost £150!

Now he was ready for Julie's cattery. At this point I didn't want her to rehome Toby for me. I just wanted her to keep him while he got used to the litter tray. In a cat pen there was not much alternative space to use as a toilet, and if he didn't use the litter tray, clearing up wouldn't be too bad.

I rang Julie to ask if she was willing to do this. 'Have you got space for him? He's not had both his vaccinations yet.'

'It's quiet at the moment, though I will be busy over

Christmas. I can put him in the quarantine pen, but you will have to come and fetch him if I suddenly need it for a customer's cat,' she said.

'I'll bring him over this afternoon.' I was now more confident about picking up Toby. As before, he merely cowered in terrified helplessness.

It isn't very far to Julie's cattery and while he was in the car, he remained silent and unmoving. When I got out of the car with the carrier, he began his despairing struggle again, throwing himself against the bars of the carrier.

Once he was released in the cat pen he huddled hunched in the cat bed. 'He looked like a ginger ragbag. He was so skinny,' Julie recalled later. 'He wasn't social. He wouldn't look me in the eye.'

He looked like a cat who had given up hope.

Chapter 3

Rescue and recovery

Poor Toby. He remained in a state of fear and depression for several days. 'He's eating well, but he's terrified,' Julie reported. 'He's still got intermittent diarrhoea but he's beginning to get used to the litter trays.'

I decided to take him to the vet again. Although it wasn't quite time for Toby's second vaccination, I was worried about his bowels.

I found Toby cowering under, rather than sitting on top of, the blanket in his bed. I picked him out of the bed and put him in his carrier. He didn't struggle. I didn't put a fleece in the carrier this time, since the last time he simply dug himself under it. This time I carried the carrier with the front towards me, so that my body blocked the sight of the outside world.

He was more subdued than the last carrier trip, when he had flung himself at the bars. This time he did not try to escape.

He was in a state of what experts call 'learned helplessness' – a cat so stressed that he was beyond reacting.

At the vet's I had to wait for about half an hour. I had brought a blanket to cover the whole carrier. This helped him a little to cope with the presence of dogs and other cats in the waiting room.

Inside the consulting room, he again crouched immobile on the vet's table. He was a cat resigned to whatever life threw at him.

I was confident that after eating about four envelopes of cat food a day he would be beginning to put on weight. To my surprise, the vet remarked, 'He has lost weight, not gained it.'

Looking at the miserable little cat, now even thinner than before, I was glad I hadn't waited longer to get veterinary help. How was it possible for him to lose weight after all that good food? He had been devouring any food he could get his paws on. For a cat who had been starving, even a single ounce lost was serious. Something must be done.

'If it was an infection, it would have shown itself by now,' said the vet.

'Could it be the stress of the cattery?' I asked.

'Maybe, but it's more likely to be digestion problems. He's eating but not absorbing the food.' She sold me a large bag of expensive prescription food, designed for cats with stomach difficulties.

Back at the cattery, Toby disappeared into the covered cat bed I had now brought for him. Totally enclosed but for the entrance, it provided a more secure place for him to hide. Inside, I had put a fleece smelling of Tilly. This was to get him used to her smell and to mingle his scent with hers. Cats identify

44

friends and foe by scent. Both Toby and Tilly would have to mix their scents into an overall family scent. That family scent profile, smelling of the two cats and the two humans in the household, would mark their core home territory, and reassure them both that they were in a familiar place.

Now Toby was completely hidden away in the covered cat bed, he should feel a little less stressed. Julie said she would give me daily reports.

I was not sure what to do next. His litter-tray use, although better, was still slightly unreliable. He had been prescribed kaolin with probiotics, as well as the new food, and I had bought some Feliway spray. This artificial calming scent, sprayed daily in his pen, should help him cope with stress. All in all, he had now cost about £300. Sometimes a rescue cat can cost as much as a pedigree kitten!

A couple of days later there was good news from the veterinary surgery. Toby had tested clear for FIV, so it would be safe to bring him home and safe to let him live with Tilly, with no danger of her catching the virus. What is more, Julie reported that his new prescription food had resulted in reliable litter-tray use.

He was dumping in the right location but still not in the correct formation! Despite the special diet and daily probiotics with kaolin, he was still suffering from intermittent diarrhoea. So, on one of my two afternoons off when I had a sitter for Ronnie, I took him back yet again to the vet.

This time Toby lost it. When I tried to get him in the cat carrier, he literally started climbing the wall of the cat pen. I grabbed a blanket, which was in the pen, and sort of pulled him off the wall with it. He had a sore nose from the struggle.

At the vet's he was very cowed. He sat hunched, but without a struggle, on the scales.

'He has put on 200 grams,' reported Sarah. I asked her, on the scale of one to ten, where she would put him. 'Well, the scale is one to nine,' she said, 'and I put him at three.' That was much higher than I expected. He was recovering, even if his recovery was slow. He was now getting goodness out of his food.

Then I noticed something odd about his behaviour in the surgery. He seemed to enjoy physical contact despite his fear. While he was sitting on the scale without moving, both Sarah and I stroked him, and I saw his front feet kneading a little bit. Somewhere under the terrified, traumatized stray was a potentially affectionate cat.

December had come and it was freezing outside. I still felt guilty about what I was putting Toby through by leaving him in the cattery but at least it was better than the street. It was now so cold that he would not have survived, both starving *and* freezing. Living on icy concrete under a car would have killed him.

No date could be fixed for his castration, because the vet judged him still to be too thin and too ill. Instead, three days of poo samples were required to check his bowel problems. Julie heroically agreed to take these and I would then deliver them to the vet. These would be tested for the giardia parasite and campylobacter bacterium, both common among stray cats. That was another £100 but I felt it was money well spent. At least Toby's problems could be cured – unlike my poor husband's cancers.

That evening, lying awake worrying about Ronnie, I had a

sudden horrible thought. What if Toby had the feline leukaemia virus rather than FIV and was going to die of this cancer of the blood cells? I'd had breast cancer the year before Toby's arrival. A three-cancer household of Ronnie, Toby and me would be just too much to bear, emotionally.

Then I reminded myself that he had tested clear for FIV, and the chances of him having FeLV were low. Rescuing Toby was *not* going to be doomed to failure. Rescuing Tilly had been a triumph, changing a terrified, scruffy cat into a loving companion. I had even lately put effort into rescuing myself from the stress of looking after Ronnie by getting more help. These rescue attempts were going fine, unlike some of my earlier rescues of people.

Rescuing is one of my character traits. I'm not very proud of this because I recognize that it doesn't proceed just from compassion on my part, but is also some kind of deep-down need. It is as much about helping myself feel better as it is about helping others, and if I'm not careful, it can get out of control.

When I was much younger, I was into rescuing people, not cats. I remember taking in a young woman who was on the run. Iggy (a pretty cool name in the 1960s) had been in care and she said she was looking for somewhere to stay, otherwise she would have to sleep rough. She was wearing a mini skirt short enough to show her knickers. Her tousled hair was streaked black and blonde with brown roots. She wasn't very clean. In the journalists' pub where I met her, there were only too many men willing to give her a bed for the night. So I thought I'd better offer her one! Better a night in my spare room than having a Hobson's choice of the blokes in the pub.

Iggy obviously had problems but as I rarely saw her,

I never discovered exactly what they were. She stayed in bed so late that I never met her in the morning and she stayed out so late that I never met her in the evening either. She was even later to arrive home than I was. She remained with me for about two weeks and then ran off with some of my nicer clothes. I never saw her again.

I guess I was a bit of a sucker for a hard-luck story. One of my colleagues told me an elaborate story of his need for an immediate £200, a very large sum in the 1960s. If I had asked around the office, I could have discovered he was a compulsive gambler and lending him money was not a good idea. He was moaning about not having enough money for his phone bill. He didn't even directly ask me for it, but at the age of 21 I was ready, willing and anxious to help.

'How much do you want? I could you lend some money,' I volunteered.

'I will pay you back,' he swore. 'Open a Post Office account for me and I'll put away twenty pounds a week.' I did and he didn't.

My biggest rescue attempt was my first husband. In the days of the movie *Blow Up* about a glossy photographer, and David Bailey and Jean Shrimpton taking up gossip space in the newspapers, even newspaper photographers had a borrowed glamour. Photographers were almost as charismatic as movie stars. So it was perhaps to be expected that I would fall in love with a photographer.

Nothing too bad in that, but the object of my passion was a fashion photographer with problems, who worked for the same newspaper as I did. He was moody and unhappy and this made him irresistible to me. He was short of money and drank too much – much too much. Oh yes, and he had a cat. That possibly added to the attraction, although in those days I preferred dogs.

I can't say he didn't warn me. 'I'm a miserable sod. You'll never change me,' he remarked once. For me, this was a challenge and I like a challenge, whether it is a miserable starving cat, like Toby, or a miserable photographer. I didn't want to change his drinking habits; I just thought I could *make* him happy.

I didn't realize then (and this was to be significant) that unless he did something about his drinking, there was no hope of any of his other problems going away. I thought he was drinking because he was unhappy. Perhaps that is what he thought, too. Now I know that he was drinking because he was addicted. Happiness or misery made no difference to his need for alcohol.

One of the many reasons why it's more fun rescuing cats than men is that cats don't drink or use drugs. Well, I suppose they take drugs in the form of catnip, but they always know when to stop. They don't become permanently hooked on it. Usually, after wriggling around a bit, sniffing the catnip mouse and looking silly, they get up and walk away. Sometimes they have an air of embarrassment about themselves but they use catnip in moderation.

They don't end up in a fight after catnip. They don't vomit. They don't fall down in the gutter. Altogether their drug use is recreational and civilized. Unlike addicts and alcoholics, they don't whinge about life. Self-pity is unknown to cats. They don't blame others for their plight.

So who wouldn't prefer rescuing cats to rescuing humans?

Cats do their best to survive and even *in extremis* may continue to be friendly to the human race that has treated them so badly. Toby, after all, had not bitten or scratched me when I picked him up, even though he clearly was terrified by the experience of his new life.

But in the days when I was rescuing miserable men, I didn't realize how relatively easy and enjoyable it was to turn to cats in their place. Indeed, even when I had taken up with my husband, Ronnie (not a rescue case), and learnt not to rescue people, I was still not very sympathetic to cats. When a small black cat fell into the basement of my London house, I merely picked it up and took it to the local RSPCA. I never thought of giving it a home. I never thought of asking what would happen to it. I did the minimum I could do for the kitten and, since in those days in the 1970s the RSPCA was overwhelmed with unwanted animals, it may not even have found a home.

The reason for this lack of caring, I think, was my own growing addiction to alcohol, which, in turn, created a growing self-centredness. Alcohol was beginning to take over my life, leaving little room for hobbies or interests other than drinking. Even my rescue impulse was blotted out when I was blotto. I worked and I drank.

Of course, I didn't admit to this. I used to say: 'I work hard and I play hard.' That phrase kept alcohol out of sight, for I didn't, couldn't or wouldn't see what the alcohol was doing to me. Addiction is the only disease (or disorder) that tells you it is not happening to you.

It should not have been like that. I was, by now, married to Ronnie, who was, and still is, the love of my life. We had run away, planning to start our life together with a holiday in

Cyprus, an escapade that started badly because I had forgotten I had lost my passport. 'I know you've got the tickets but I don't see how I can come,' I admitted. 'I forgot to get a new one.'

With a lofty air of *savoir faire*, Ronnie said, 'I'll get the Foreign Office to do you an emergency one. We've got a few hours before we need to be at the airport after all.' I didn't believe he could do this.

I was impressed when, about an hour later, after he had made a couple of phone calls, we went round to the Passport Office in Westminster. 'Miss Haddon is my researcher,' he explained to the young man at the Foreign Office who was on duty in charge of passport emergencies that evening. How he had wheedled his way into the office after it closed, I did not ask. While we sat there, and I tried not to giggle, the young man went off and got me an emergency passport. The next day we were in the Ledra Palace Hotel in Nicosia, drinking whisky sours in between swimming, laughing and making love.

I loved him for this amazing ability to get into places where most people could not go – the mark of a fine journalist. I loved him for his bravery. During a long life as a war correspondent, not only had he been close to shot and shell, but he had also once been kidnapped by Algerian terrorists and locked in a garage.

'I thought I was going to be killed,' he said. 'I talked my way out, helped by giving them every bit of money I had on me.' Then he calmly walked back to his hotel and cabled (all done by cable in those days) his story to the newspaper, playing down his narrow escape rather than bigging it up.

Perhaps because he had been a Royal Marine in his youth during World War Two, he considered it bad form to boast about narrow escapes. He was more likely to joke about them. Some journalists boast about the shot and shell falling around them, but most war reporters generally agree that this is beneath the dignity of a good correspondent. War reporters do take casualties, although obviously not as many as fighting soldiers. I can think of three friends who have died while covering wars. So I loved Ronnie for his courage.

I loved him for his wit and the way he could tell a good story – great craic, as the Irish say. He was a wonderful raconteur and I cannot retell his stories in the way he told them. Often he made me laugh out loud.

If ever a woman should have been happy, it should have been me. I loved Ronnie. I was loved. I enjoyed my work for a colour magazine. I had friends. I had enough money. Admittedly, I didn't have children; nor did I have a cat. Yet many people live contented lives without children and some even lead happy lives without cats.

And yet … something was wrong.

I knew there was something abnormal about me. I didn't *want* children. I didn't even *want* a cat. I think that subconsciously I knew that I wouldn't be able to look after either. While I was drinking, I was not a fit person to be a mother – or a fit person to be a cat owner, come to that. Animals who are kept by alcoholics often have a hard time of it. The dogs wear an anxious look. The cats, more sensible in their relationship with damaged humans, often just pack up and leave home.

My drinking didn't seem *that* bad, of course – or so I told myself. Of course I drank too much; all journalists did. When Ronnie was at home, we would both go to the famous Fleet

Street bar El Vino and drink large whiskies until it closed. Then we would go home and have a meal or go out to a restaurant and have a bottle of wine between us. Afterwards, it was sometimes a whisky nightcap for him and always a whisky nightcap or two or three for me.

Earlier, of course, both of us would usually have had a boozy Fleet Street lunch with colleagues, including about half a bottle of wine each, sometimes more. Journalists worked hard and played even harder in those days. My drinking certainly didn't show up as particularly bad among the hard-drinking crowd that I mingled with.

'Though I did wonder a bit,' said Ronnie, years later, 'when you polished off half a bottle of pear brandy at the end of the evening once.' At the time, he said nothing. He knew my character, which was to pick a fight if he made any criticism (a fault that, I am ashamed to say, I still have, although I try not to react nowadays). He was very laid back, a relaxed man who let people go their own way, a man strong enough not to need to control a woman.

It was when he was away, reporting on wars, revolutions and foreign affairs, that my drinking took its true toll. At the start of the evening I could not predict what would happen to me or what I would do. If I woke up, or came to, in my own bed, I would have a huge sense of relief. This relief was tempered by the possibility that I was not alone. If I was with somebody, did I know them or was it a complete stranger? If I was alone, then another surge of relief would sweep through me.

Sometimes I would start drinking in a Fleet Street pub with newspaper friends and acquaintances, and stay there until the pub closed. There was always somebody to drink with.

Journalists in those days worked in shifts that went on into the early hours of the morning. At different times, they would come off shift and go for a drink. So I could drink all evening with a shifting cast of colleagues.

In those days, almost all of the newspaper offices were within walking distance of each other, and Fleet Street was a community of tribes, each one from a different newspaper. Each pub had its regulars. The White Swan, known as 'The Mucky Duck', and the back bar of The Harrow (the front bar was for printers) were the *Daily Mail* journalists' pubs. The King and Keys and The Falstaff were the *Daily Telegraph* pubs. The White Hart, known as 'The Stab in the Back', was the *Daily Mirror* pub, while the *Express* guys drank at The Albion.

Plenty of journalists drank far too much, but I was one of the ones who got addicted. Sometimes I regained consciousness in a strange house, not my own home. In the early hours of the morning I would stagger out into the London streets, looking for a street name that would tell me where I was. Sometimes I couldn't remember how I had got there or what had happened to me during the evening. I was too ashamed to ask my drinking buddies any details. It was best not to know.

Occasionally, there would be clues to what had occurred, like the morning when I woke in my own bed. Where had I been? I found a matchbox from the Playboy Club and had a fragmentary recollection of a Playboy bunny serving me some food. As I wasn't a member of the Playboy Club, somebody must have taken me there. I looked in my purse. I cannot have gambled because there was plenty of money in it. To this day, I do not know who took me there or why.

It was always comforting to be in the company of other

heavy drinkers. Misery loves company; so does addiction. I remember an evening that began in El Vino, when I was out with an eminent political journalist and an equally eminent literary editor. We went on to a restaurant for supper. In the morning the literary editor rang up to ask, 'Do you know who paid for the meal? All I can remember is that you and I were too drunk to write a cheque.'

'I can't remember,' I had to admit. 'It's a bit of a blur.' This was a polite way of admitting that I'd had a complete alcoholic blackout, or alcoholic loss of memory. I didn't remember the name of the restaurant. But the phone call was immensely reassuring. 'Phew,' I thought, 'it wasn't just me making a fool of myself.'

I was a 'Shall I hit him or screw him?' drunk. Very belligerent. I did hit Ronnie once. We were having an argument and I was shouting at him. I moved towards him and beat him several times on the chest with first one fist and then the other. It was a tribute to his control that he did not hit me back. He merely lifted me off the ground and shook me. 'Stop this,' he said in a quiet voice. And I did.

Looking back, I can never understand why he didn't leave me. Instead, he looked after me when he was at home, on occasion stopping the car so that I could be sick in the gutter. He would take me home when it was clear that I was about to fall over. He would offer to fight people, protecting me, if they objected to my loud-mouthed swearing in the pub. He never criticized my appalling behaviour.

Why? Maybe he just loved me.

Maybe it was something to do with his attitude to life. He was quietly cynical or, perhaps I should say, realistic. He believed that people did what they did and giving advice unasked for would be a waste of energy and time. He had spent 20 years as a Paris correspondent, before I met him, and he had adopted the worldly French attitude to sex and marriage.

After all, I was his third wife and he was my second husband. Neither of us were saints, and neither of us had a good grasp of the concept of lifelong marriage. Perhaps sexual fidelity was not the most important feature to the much-married, like us. Courtesy, kindness and companionship seemed more important to both of us.

Even in these I was falling short, however. I had become intensely selfish, rude and sometimes downright unkind. One incident, of many, shows how my behaviour towards the man I loved (and I really did love him) was deteriorating.

Ronnie had been in Oman, reporting on the terrorism that then afflicted that country. With a party of journalists he was taken by helicopter to an area where the British SAS were helping out the Sultan's own forces. On their return the helicopter crashed into the desert.

'I thought of you when we were going down in circles, and tried to write a note saying I loved you,' he told me later.

Luckily for the passengers, nobody died. All of them got out alive, but all of them had back injuries. Ronnie's was particularly severe so he had to be airlifted out by the RAF back to the then RAF hospital in Wiltshire. I went to visit him there and after a few days he was transferred to the King Edward VII Hospital in central London. I visited most days for the first two weeks, but then heard the unwelcome news that he was likely to be there for another month.

'I don't think I'll visit you any more,' I told him. 'It's too boring sitting here. I'll see you when you get home.'

The recollection of my unkindness still makes me cringe. For the next month, I continued to party every evening, ignoring my husband in his hospital bed. I wasn't going to let his illness interfere with my drinking. Alcohol was now more important than anything else, including the husband whom I loved and who loved me. I needed alcohol regularly more than I needed to spend time with Ronnie.

He would not have been too unhappy in his hospital bed at the King Edward VII Hospital for Officers, as it was still known then. The regime on the ward, which he shared with three other middle-aged men, one of them a wine merchant, was very relaxed. Champagne for lunch was kept in the ward sister's fridge, and at 6pm sleeping pills and ice, to go with the Scotch, were handed out to all four of them.

However, having no visits from me, he decided to make a trip to El Vino in Fleet Street to see his chums. Somehow, he persuaded the hospital to transport him there and he was wheeled into El Vino on a stretcher. 'That had never happened before or since,' recalled El Vino's chairman. I discovered about this escapade later. I was too busy getting drunk elsewhere to know about it at the time.

Just as well I didn't have a cat in those days. If I could treat my husband like that, who knows what I would have done to a cat. Ronnie stayed with me, but I think any sensible cat would have left home.

My other interests began to fall away. I didn't read much. As my evenings were full of drinking, there wasn't much time. I didn't watch TV much for the same reason. I had started to take an interest in early classical music a few years earlier, but that went, too. I didn't really have hobbies or interests. Apart from work, my life was in the pub.

And so it went on. My behaviour became more and more erratic. One evening I woke up with blood pouring from my elbows and gravel in the wounds. I did not know how it had happened. A passing neighbour told me the following day that she had found me lying in the gutter howling and had kindly helped me to my feet, opened the front door with my keys and put me to bed to sleep it off.

I had no recollection of any of this, being in an alcoholic blackout. Again. What had I done to cause these wounds on my elbows? I could not know. I began to be frightened at my lack of self-control. If I could do this to myself, what else might I do?

I decided to consult Fleet Street's most celebrated drunken woman journalist. Mandy drank astonishing amounts of whisky and would be found in Fleet Street or Soho pubs every lunchtime and every evening. When the pubs closed in the afternoon, as they did in those days, she would often move up from Fleet Street to The Wig and Pen, an afternoon drinking club frequented by drunk barristers from the nearby law courts. On leaving The Wig and Pen, Mandy was sometimes so drunk that she could be seen crawling down Fleet Street before hoisting herself up on to a bar stool in the pub of her choice.

So consulting Mandy seemed a safe thing to do. She wasn't going to be judgmental. She would understand. I asked her to lunch and we ate some lunch and drank more than we ate. I spilled the beans to her how I was out of control when Ronnie was abroad, how I couldn't be sure of getting home, and how I couldn't be sure of getting home alone.

'But aren't you happy with him?' was her response. I told

her that I was. 'Then how can you behave to him like that? He's such a lovely man.'

Far from being understanding, it was clear that Mandy was shocked. And if Mandy, of all people, was shocked, what did that say about my behaviour? That lunch edged me further towards despair. It also edged me towards recovery.

A little trickle of hope came from something I was writing. The Salvation Army in the UK were celebrating their hundredth anniversary and I was assigned to cover it. I went to their headquarters and heard about their work. I read their founder's book, *In Darkest England*, and I discovered that all Salvation Army officers had to sign the pledge not to drink alcohol. I was touched by the officers' evident commitment and kindness to others, so different from my selfish drinking. The contrast between their way of life and mine was startling.

A few days later, during some weeks when Ronnie was abroad, I surpassed myself in how much I drank and how badly behaved I was in public. The guilt and shame of it seemed intolerable and only by drinking again could I get rid of it. I could not live with my drinking self and I could not live without alcohol. I drank to get rid of guilt and shame and then my drinking caused further guilt and shame.

One night, crawling into bed, I collapsed into a fitful sleep. I woke in the early hours of an April morning to hear a blackbird singing in our street. Listening to the song was like some kind of revelation.

'I must stop drinking,' I thought. 'If I am to keep this wonderful husband of mine, I must clean up my act. Completely. I can't control what happens to me when I drink. I can't control how much I drink. I must give up alcohol altogether.'

Chapter 4

Sobriety and a stray cat

On the first day of my new life I felt really ill. I couldn't eat breakfast. I just made myself a cup of tea with sugar and started the slow process of getting over the hangover.

I must have still been drunk from the night before. I had to go down the stairs from bedroom to kitchen holding the banister tightly so I didn't fall down the stairs. At the kitchen table, I sat nursing the tea. My hands shook so badly I couldn't take it back upstairs with me. After drinking a second cup I felt able to go back upstairs (less likely to trip upwards) and run the bath.

The bath was the beginning of cleaning up my act. I washed away the smell of alcohol from my pores. I threw my clothes of the night before into the clothes' basket for washing. I put on clean clothes and went downstairs to sit at my desk.

This was an awful hangover, but not the worst I'd had.

During other hangovers I had been too dizzy even to take my head off the pillow in the morning. I wasn't sick into the lavatory pan, as sometimes I was. This morning, as I sat at my desk, I could remember what I had done the evening before. Indeed, I wished that the memory was not so clear. An alcoholic blackout would have been better than a memory that filled me with more shame and guilt.

My hangovers, as well as my drinking, had been getting worse. At times, I would be so hung over that getting to work involved a prolonged and nauseous journey. I would start by taking my normal bus, then have to get off it because I felt so sick. With luck, fresh air and walking a bit would make me feel slightly better and I would get the next bus, only to have to get off that one, too. There was a difference, however, about this hangover. Something about the moment when the blackbird sang had given me resolve to get help. Yes, I felt the familiar feelings of guilt and shame, but this time the despair was mingled with resolve to change my ways.

I will do something. I will not take a drink today.

That moment when shame and fear turn into the decision to change is when a drinking alcoholic decides to choose life over death. Alcoholism has been called slow suicide, a description that some people might think exaggerated. It is not. I still mourn the loss of friends who did not survive their addiction – Diana, who killed herself in despair with a grisly overdose of paracetamol; Helen, who hanged herself in her garage while her child was staying with her grandmother; Pauline, who died in her flat and lay there for a month before being discovered by the authorities.

Addiction seems to override the instinct to survive, an

instinct that animals share with us. Animals do not commit suicide, unlike humans. Their desire to live is stronger, and perhaps simpler, than ours. From under the cars, terrified Toby had emerged into Gaynor's garden to eat the hedgehog food. People talk of the triumph of the human spirit, as if humans had the monopoly of courage. I see in animals a similar triumph over adversity, when a desire to survive overcomes pain and fear.

I once glimpsed a stray cat in London, coming out of a basement of the huge Department of the Environment block, a concrete monster of a building erected in the 1960s and now pulled down. The stray was a tabby, holding up a broken paw, going about its business on three legs, trying to survive on food from dustbins and litter.

The image of that wounded cat has haunted me ever since. I went back to the basement and put out cat food but it wasn't eaten. I don't know what happened to that cat. Was it run over? Was it picked up by a friendly human? Did it survive a few more days before dying of starvation and pain? I shall never know.

If a mere stray cat can force itself to live, despite a broken and untreated front paw, who are we humans to complain about our lives? My troubles with alcohol had been of my own making. In that, the stray cats I have helped have been my moral superiors, being innocent yet afflicted with real hardships.

But my drinking *had* taken me to the point where I had to admit I was an alcoholic and could not fall lower – in my own eyes. So I knew what it felt like to be at the lowest ebb.

There was a way out for me. Thirty-four years before Toby turned up in my life, I gave up drinking and decided to be a good wife to Ronnie.

A few days later, a black and white cat, Fat Ada, turned up

in my garden shed with her kitten. Giving up alcohol had made me fit to be a cat owner, so after finding a home for her kitten, she became the first cat of my adult life.

I had peered in the garden shed and discovered a large black and white cat settled snugly in an old cardboard box with a single kitten. She had lined the box with her fur (as I found out later) and was taking good care of her kitten. Each time I came near she would chirrup at it, calling it close to her.

I had to go to the newsagent to buy some cat food, as there was understandably none in the house. I put some food down on a saucer and it was clear the cat was hungry. She rose from the box and ate it all, glancing sideways at me but content to do this in my presence. On impulse I picked her up and carried her into the house in my arms, then I went back for the kitten.

The next stage was to go to the local pet shop and buy a cat bed. This she refused to use. She decided she and the kitten would make their headquarters under the kitchen sink, just near the waste pipe. So I put the bed there and there she stayed for the next few weeks.

I hadn't planned to have a cat and indeed I didn't feel I needed one. It started with feeding her and became a series of small steps towards cat owning – first feeding, then bringing her and the kitten into the kitchen, then arranging his adoption and her spaying. At none of these stages was I aware that she was going to change my life.

Sometimes I feel that the arrival of Ada at that particular time was more than a coincidence. Perhaps Ada (for she became fat as well as happy) was a reward for sobriety. As I struggled to stay sober, she brought joy to my life. Was it the first step to being addicted to cats? Perhaps. Fat Ada helped me to step away from my previous life as a drunk.

However, stopping drinking alcohol in any form whatsoever for week after week was surprisingly unpleasant. It had been part of my social life – almost all meals except breakfast had been accompanied with wine and often preceded by a couple of whiskies. Alcohol helped me relax. Alcohol helped me keep going when I was tired. Alcohol helped me enjoy myself.

The first three months of a sober life were particularly difficult. I was tired all the time. My memory was affected. I would be taking the London underground and suddenly realize I did not know where I was going or why. I used to have to get off the train and sit on a bench until the memory came back and I could proceed on my journey.

Ordinary drinkers who can control how much and when they drink will probably think I was making an unnecessary fuss. People who have given up cigarettes, sometimes more than once, will understand what is involved. The craving for a drink was most intense when I was emotionally upset – angry or fearful. It became clear to me that stopping drinking was the easy part; the difficult part was not starting again. With help from other people recovering from alcoholism, I persisted.

During those first few months, a moment occurred that some people would call a spiritual awakening – not a religious moment but one that lit up my inner spirit. I was looking out of the window at a Somerset wood a field away from me. Ronnie and I had walked in that wood when it was carpeted with bluebells and I had marvelled at its beauty. Now it was autumn and the leaves on the trees were turning to gold and crimson before they died and fell.

At that moment, I had a glimpse of time and my small place in it. The leaves were beautiful because they were transient. It was the oncoming of their death that made them turn to gold and crimson. Transience, the way nothing lasts for ever, was the secret of their beauty. Those whom I loved, both human and feline, and I myself, were part of that transience, the mutability of lives that must end in death. My feeling was one of joyful acceptance. At that moment, and only for that moment, which I cannot now recapture, I accepted my part in life with its inevitable journey towards my death.

Perseverance with not drinking paid huge rewards. The love between Ronnie and me increased. Both of us had to get used to the idea that Ronnie would spend some of his time enjoying craic and whisky with his friends in El Vino, while I would not be accompanying him any more. It wasn't that I didn't love him, just that I didn't want to spend too much time around alcohol. He had the right to enjoy drinking with friends and wine with meals, while I had lost that privilege.

Once I was sober enough to notice what was going on around me, I began to appreciate even more the courage of the foreign correspondents like Ronnie. True, they did not take part in battle, and during conventional wars they were usually helped by the military of whatever side they were reporting on. They did not, like the photographers, have to be right in the front line. But nonetheless there were dangers.

Getting killed, of course, was not their aim. Getting killed has the severe disadvantage that you do not get your story out. So, successful foreign correspondents took risks but not for the sake of excitement. When Ronnie was in his prime, relaying a story to his newspaper involved cable, telex and phones (the story was dictated to a human copytaker back at the office). Now satellite communications make filing a story easier, but you still have to be alive to report.

I knew three war reporters who were killed in the course of their work – Bruce Piggott, a young Australian reporter working for Reuters, killed in Vietnam in 1965; Marie Colvin, a wonderfully daring and dashing woman, killed in Homs in 2012 during the Syrian civil war; and Nicholas Tomalin, editor of the section where I worked at the *Sunday Times*, who went to the Yom Kippur war of 1973, where he was killed by a Syrian missile.

Ronnie was reporting the Yom Kippur war, too, with his friend and co-writer Christopher Dobson. Their two-man reportage had been so cutting edge and extensive that they had beaten, or at least been equal to, newspapers that had sent as many as six journalists. I still have a photo of him and Chris with General Ariel 'Arik' Sharon.

Being invited to the General's tent was a journalistic coup. Sharon described how the battles had been going and what he planned to do next. His wife was sending him a regular hamper from their farm in Israel and he shared Scotch and various goodies with them.

'General, you keep a very tidy battlefield,' Ronnie said to him, over a whisky. Typical chutzpah from a journalist, but Ronnie had some officer training and had seen action in World War Two as a Royal Marine. Sharon merely laughed.

War reporters form a gang of their own. From different newspapers and different countries, they converge on wars, revolutions and riots. Naturally, they get to know each other. Through Ronnie, I met this gang of élite reporters – Hilary

Brown, a statuesque blonde from the American Broadcasting Corporation, who was frequently seen urging her cameraman and sound man to get closer to the action; Count Paolo Filo della Torre, author of a book with the splendid title of *Margaret Thatcher: La Bambola di Ferro* or, in translation, *Mrs Thatcher: Iron Baby Doll*; Bob Woodward, best known for his exposure of Nixon's dirty tricks, made into the movie *All the President's Men*; Michael Nicholson and other TV reporters, many not well known to the public but admired by their contemporaries. Thanks to Ronnie, I was on the fringes of this exciting world.

Among themselves, the foreign correspondents know who is a good reporter and who just gives the impression of being a good reporter. They do not admire big-footers, those TV presenters or 'star' feature writers who fly in and report from the hotel lobby.

'I remember one whose way of being first with the story was to read the newspaper cuttings on the plane, sit in his hotel room and write his story, then dictate it to his newspaper before going out to look at what was going on,' recalls Chris Dobson, Ronnie's co-writer on many books. 'There are also the foreign correspondents who just make it up. They are known and universally hated by their competitors.'

It was pointless to worry when Ronnie disappeared to a trouble spot. Just like a cat who disappears out of the cat flap, he would probably land on his feet and find his way home eventually.

The nearest I got to being fearful was when he was reporting on the invasion of Cyprus by the Turks. The hotel he always stayed in, the Ledra Palace, where we had spent our first runaway night together (the true honeymoon, I always thought), was bombed. There was no online news in those days to find out what was going on, but when I heard nothing more, I assumed it meant he was OK and off in the field somewhere. I assumed correctly. Four days later, one of the TV reporters coming back to London, dropped off a letter for me. It started 'Darling Celia …' I have never read the rest of it. His writing was so bad, I could only pick out the occasional word! But I still treasure the love letter I cannot read.

As well as covering wars and revolutions, Ronnie and Chris Dobson were becoming acknowledged experts on terrorism, among the first. They wrote about four different books on the subject. I, meanwhile, was busy staying sober, looking after my first adult cat and writing a column about pets for the *Daily Telegraph*. Both of us were developing our specialities. The contrast between his outgoing interests and my animal ones could not have been more marked.

Our lives diverged professionally and personally but the rubber-band effect kept us together. We snapped back together at every opportunity. His return was like a honeymoon. And I never forgot, and never will, that this brave, strong man hadn't left me during the years I was in the grip of addiction. He would have been justified in walking out on me then. He stayed.

Just as I had little interest in terrorism, so Ronnie had little interest in cats. After I sobered up, he had to become accustomed to the cats that now came into my life. It wasn't his fault that he was indifferent to animals. He had been brought up without any pets. As a child, he never had so much as a rabbit or a hamster. There was no family dog, no family cat, not even a family budgie.

He didn't dislike animals; he just felt that keeping a cat or a dog, or even a budgie, would interfere with his primary purpose in life, which was to be ready to drop everything and catch a plane to the next trouble spot. He was responsible enough to know that taking in an animal was a big commitment. So if I wanted a cat, I, not he, was responsible for it. We argued over this. Several years later, he would even clean the litter tray! So I guess I won the argument.

His first close encounter with a cat had been about two years before Ada arrived in our lives. We had a country cottage in Somerset where we spent weekends. The local farmer kindly allowed Ronnie to take a gun on to his land. I don't think Ronnie ever shot anything – there wasn't really anything much to shoot. However, each time Ronnie set out with a gun, the local farm cat, Juffy, would accompany him.

Juffy was a neutered tomcat. His original name was a Somerset version of Jouffe, the French name of a type of wheat. He was so called because his fur was pale ginger, rather like the colour of ripened corn. He was fed daily but otherwise received no extra care. He lived in the farm buildings, not in the house. His function was to kill rats and mice, which he did with great efficiency. Each morning, the farmer's wife would open her front door to find several corpses strewn on the concrete path.

Juffy was never taken to the vet, except for one trip to castrate him. He wasn't vaccinated, but since he lived in the country in a small hamlet of five houses with only one other cat, an elderly female, his chances of catching a disease were limited.

He certainly looked perfectly healthy. He must have had worms and fleas, but these, or their effects, were not visible. As he never came into the house, the farmer's wife wasn't concerned about them. Probably, the parasites lived in a kind of balance, their numbers low enough to allow him to flourish. Cats who are completely covered in fleas are normally starving or ill, too ill to limit flea numbers by grooming them off.

His lifestyle wasn't a bad one. He was typical of the farm cats that have lived with humans for thousands of years. There were plenty of farm buildings to shelter in during wet or windy weather, with hay or straw to snuggle deep in during cold weather. He had regular meals from his owner, topped up by rodents, a diet to which his system was perfectly adjusted by years of evolution.

He had the rich pleasure of being able fully to express his instinct to hunt. For cats, hunting mice is what experts call 'species-specific behaviour'. It is what they are designed to do and a supreme pleasure for them, a pleasure denied to cats who live entirely indoors.

Juffy was a confident cat. In warm weather, he would lie in the middle of the road soaking up the sun and the warmth from the tarmac. Luckily, the road was almost deserted. The occasional motorist would stop and honk the car's horn at him. With slow dignity, Juffy would get to his feet and stalk off to the side, allowing the car to pass.

He was also relaxed around cows. The farmer's main crop was beef bullocks, produced in an old-fashioned way without artificial insemination. Trumpeter, his quiet and aimiable bull, would mate with the Aberdeen Angus cows. Their calves would be brought up naturally in the fields by their mothers (unlike modern calves, which are separated from birth). The females might be incorporated into the herd, and the males were sold off when they reached a certain weight.

Juffy was completely without fear of them. If his daily

territory inspection took him across the fields, the cows, and even more so the calves, would cluster round him in curiosity. Juffy would usually sit down and wash himself in the midst of them. If a bovine muzzle came too close, he would give it a smart scratch and continue his toilet.

Naturally, Juffy visited our cottage to see what was going on. He took a particular interest in our company at meal times and was rewarded, by me, with some food. Perhaps because of the worms, he never grew fat despite being fed by two households. In warm weather, he would sleep in a gardener's basket in our porch.

Even though I was the one who fed him, Juffy preferred Ronnie. He would follow Ronnie round the garden at a distance of about three feet. He enjoyed sitting idly, watching Ronnie's labours in cultivating the garden. He followed him on walks, mewing plaintively if he felt Ronnie had gone too far from the farm. Three fields from the house was the extent of Juffy's territory. For the pleasure of Ronnie's company he would go a fourth field but would complain loudly at every step. At five fields, he would stop dead, still mewing, and watch Ronnie continue into the distance before turning for home.

His real delight was when Ronnie went out with his gun. Juffy was clever enough to know that, with a gun, Ronnie would not go too far, just round the fields that belonged to the farmer. So he would set off rather like a Labrador dog, about three paces behind Ronnie. If Ronnie started without him, Juffy would gallop across the field to catch him up.

'It's embarrassing,' Ronnie said. 'I look such a fool going out shooting with a cat.' But he was fully sensitive of the honour.

Would Juffy have actually *retrieved* for Ronnie? I feel it is unlikely. He was such a confident cat that perhaps he would not have run away from a gun shot, but I cannot see him actually carrying home a pheasant (not that there were any). A rabbit? Perhaps. He certainly killed and ate the local rabbits, as well as the rats and mice. I used to come across the occasional rabbit scut or foot, discarded from one of his meals.

Juffy softened up Ronnie for Ada, our first proper cat. I credit Juffy with first awakening Ronnie's admiration of cats. So when Ada just turned up with her kitten in the garden shed, after initially threatening, 'Either that cat goes or I go,' Ronnie had settled down to life with her. He used to sing 'Abide with me' to her, affecting to believe that she was a devoted hymn singer. She was company for me when he was away at some trouble spot.

Just how much he had grown to love her was clear when the end came. Ada had been losing weight. She was a portly cat and for a time I didn't notice the change in her. This seems ridiculous to me now, but I had not had a cat entirely of my own before her arrival. I did notice that her claws seemed longer, but did not realize that this was purely because she had lost weight on her pads. Once I did realize it, I vaguely decided that her weight loss was due to her growing older.

When she got cat 'flu despite having been vaccinated, I merely thought it was bad luck or possibly a new strain of the illness. The vet I took her to, not my current vet, did not notice anything amiss, either. In those days, vets knew a great deal more about dogs than they knew about cats, and treated cats rather like second-class dogs.

With the wisdom of hindsight and more knowledge, I now realize that Ada's immune system was breaking down. In her days on the street, she had been mated and it was probably sex that had given her the Feline Immunodeficiency Virus. FIV is spread by blood, sexual fluids and saliva. When tomcats mate, they hold down the female with a bite at the nape of the neck. This bite from an infected tom, and perhaps simultaneous sexual penetration, had probably given her the virus. For Ada, love had brought death.

I had adopted her shortly after she had given birth and had her spayed. She had lived for a further six years. The virus stays dormant for several years before causing illness. In those days, there was no test for FIV, and therefore no way of knowing if a cat had the virus. Indeed, very little was known about the disease at all. HIV, or Human Immunodeficiency Virus, had been identified just a little while before Ada fell ill.

In retrospect, I grieve more for her than for any of my other cats. I was so slow to recognize her illness. She seemed to sit immobile for longer but I thought she was getting older. Now I know that hours of sitting immobile mean that a cat is in pain. Ada probably had cancer. My ignorance let her suffer for too long. For cats with cancer, there is an escape that is denied to human cancer sufferers. We make humans live out their lives to the bitter, the very bitter, end. Animals are allowed a release from their pain.

With a heavy heart, I took Ada to the vet for the last time. I went alone to his surgery in Belgravia, because Ronnie, who had seen people die in front of his eyes in battle, couldn't face seeing her death. It was proof, if I needed it, that he cared for this cat. That morning, I foolishly fed her a favourite meal of raw rabbit meat.

'I'll give her a whiff of gas,' said the vet, anxious to save her fear and pain. He loved all animals and his household included unwanted dogs and cats that he had rescued from premature euthanasia. But instead of sedating her, the gas made her choke and vomit. I had to hold her while she was sick.

'Did you feed her this morning?' he asked. 'She should not have had anything to eat.'

I had to confess that I *had* fed her. His plan to sedate and calm her before the death injection was now ruined. I had thought to be kind with that last breakfast, but I had been cruel instead. As she was choking and vomiting up that last meal, he put the final injection into her body.

It was horrible. Horrible for me and horrible for her. And it was a revelation to me.

Deaths had happened in my family but I had been shielded from them. I had never seen anybody or anything die. My parents had kept me away from the deathbeds of my grandmothers. I did not even know what had killed them; nor had I been at the deathbed of my aunt, my mother's sister, Nancy, a heavy smoker, who died of lung cancer.

Somehow, the cats of my childhood had failed to teach me much about death. I had never been to the vet for the last time to see them euthanazed. My father had sometimes shot the ailing family dogs, saying this was easier for them than a stressful visit to the vet. Unwanted kittens had probably been drowned, as the custom still was in the 1950s, and the family white rabbit, Snowdrop, had probably met her end by having her neck broken.

We children were not encouraged to ask about the manner of these deaths. We were kept away from them and all was silence. We were expected to shed a few tears and then stop talking about it. It was a time when people didn't talk about either sex or death.

People buy cats and dogs, and allow them to have kittens and puppies, so that their children can learn about sex and birth. Nobody buys a child a pet so that the child can learn about death, but perhaps they ought to.

So I was altogether ignorant of death until Ada needed to be put down. I did not know that dying, for both cats and humans, can be a difficult journey. Just as the passage into life can be painful, so can the passage out of life. Ada's death, struggling in my arms, choking on the anaesthetic while being injected for the last time, was the first death I had witnessed.

My reaction to her death was anger and fury. Fury that she had not had the allotted 12 or so years that could be expected for a well-cared for pet cat. Fury that her life had been cut short. Fury that God had allowed her to suffer in this way. She didn't deserve an early death. It just wasn't fair. I refused to accept it could happen like this.

Our six years with Ada, during which she had turned me, and even Ronnie, into a cat lover, were also six years of sobriety. I had learned how to enjoy life without alcohol. I had re-learned my marriage, discovering that I was even happier with Ronnie when I didn't drink and didn't have to live with a permanent feeling of guilt and shame. I had also learned to let him enjoy alcohol with his friends.

Ada's death really upset me. I guess I had known her better than I had known my grandmothers or my aunt. I hadn't been close to them at all. I was close to Ada. I felt anger that FIV had taken her life unduly early, that she hadn't had the full lifespan of a happy pet. I was so angry that I would regularly berate God for it in prayers that were like a string of insults to whatever higher power there may be.

When Ada died, I felt enormous guilt that I had not realized earlier how ill she was, and I knew one quick and easy way to feel better – a drink. If I went back to drinking, all this guilt would disappear. I could blot out my feelings by just pouring a large Scotch.

I didn't do it.

Instead, I lived through it without the comfort of the bottle. It was agony to clean and put away her food bowls. I shed tears as I washed the cat bed on the landing, into which she would insert her portly body each night. I put it and her food bowls out of sight in a cupboard. It was even agony to vacuum the last visible cat hairs off the carpets and think that I would never ever again complain of her fallen hair. My mother had painted a portrait of her, as she sat on a stump of wood in our garden, and for a few weeks I turned the picture to the wall. I couldn't bear to look at it.

When I came home, I would open the door expecting to see her, and my heart lurched when I realized that I would no longer be greeted by her chirrup and the tail-up signal. I still saw her sometimes out of the corner of my eye. I would turn to get a better look and find nothing there. I felt her presence every day.

For six months, I lived without a cat. It seemed disrespectful to get another one, as if I could just *replace* my black and white portly Ada with any substitute.

If anybody had said to me, 'Get another cat,' I would probably have hit them.

Yet that's what I did.

Chapter 5

Fat Little Moq and an agonizing vigil

The photo showed a black and white mother cat tenderly nursing four little black kittens. My friend Penny, who has known me since we used to make mud pies in the farmyard together, had sent it to me. As every cat owner knows, it is not always easy to find good homes for kittens, particularly not all-black ones. What better way to get them off your hands than to send a photo. Who can resist a photo of kittens?

Penny and David had adopted a black and white cat in Wales from a place in Ogogoronwy. They named her Eronwy, dropping the Ogogo from the place name! She and some other cats had been kept on a vegetarian diet, but because they could supplement it by mousing, had not suffered too much from this eccentric feeding. They were skinny but healthy.

'Eronwy was gentle and shy and a great mother,' recalls Penny. 'I just loved the way she called to me to ask for midwife services, which involved providing a cosy box for her beside me and stroking her until the first kitten arrived. Then she would be busy with the kittens, purring all the time. She was so lovely I let her have fifteen kittens.'

With that number to find homes for, it was no wonder Penny was actively enticing her friends to take one by showing them photos of the kittens.

'Ronnie, look at this photo. Penny has kittens,' I said over supper. It was rather a good supper, consisting of Lancashire hot pot, one of his favourite dishes. I was anxious to draw his attention to the photo while he was in a good mood. Had he come home grumpy I would not have raised the topic. He had finally accepted and grown to care for Ada, but I feared his idea of freedom from responsibilities at home might overcome his very moderate desire for another cat!

'I know what this is,' he replied. 'I know what you and Penny are up to.'

'They are so adorable, Ronnie. You'd love a kitten. I know you would.'

This blatant misreading of the partner's emotional state was part of my management strategy. On tricky ground, the way forward was to take a very positive step. But would it work?

'I told her we would go over this Saturday and have a look,' I said, putting as much emotional warmth into my voice as I could. Tone of voice is so important, whether training dogs, calling cats or managing partners!

'I suppose we could,' he said.

Then I dropped the subject. I like to think that he was

agreeing not only because he loved me, but also because he accepted the possibility, if not the probability, that he might find a kitten amusing. Either way, it was the go-ahead. We went to look at the kittens and came home with one. What other outcome could there have been?

Little Mog wasn't a rescue cat. She had come from a good human home and was therefore physically and emotionally healthy.

That night I went to bed with Little Mog, rather than Ronnie, in my arms. 'She is so tiny and she will miss her mother,' I told him.

'You are putting that kitten before *me*,' he exclaimed half in fun and half serious. 'It bodes ill.'

Sharing not the outside but the inside of the bed with Little Mog was my first mistake with a new kitten. From then on, she always slept inside the bed with me. She became adept at changing her position when I moved in my sleep. I would feel her climbing over my body, so as to find a new location near my arms, not my back, when I turned over. When she was a kitten, I was frightened of squashing her by mistake. It never happened. She seemed able to predict my movements and adjust her sleeping location to them.

There was, however, a huge disadvantage. Snuggling up near me inside the bed was Little Mog's way of being comforted in times of stress. This meant, therefore, that if she felt ill, she would crawl into bed. Occasionally, if she had eaten something unwise, she would crawl into bed with me in order to vomit.

Many cat owners have cursed when they got out of bed to put their bare foot on a neat little sicked-up furball. In Mog's case, the furball would be deposited level with my chest inside the bed. Since then, I have never encouraged my cats to sleep inside the sheets.

My second mistake was to play rough games with her using my fingers. She was so tiny that I could not resist it. I would wiggle my fingers and she would pounce on them, sometimes with her tiny little claws out and sometimes with a tiny little nip. I would roll her on her back and she would play fight back with claws and teeth. The tiny kitten teeth didn't hurt.

Six months later, the adult teeth and claws hurt badly. She played, as she had been taught by me, with claws out and with teeth at the ready. I began to have hands covered in semi-healed scratches.

So savage was her play that I had to adopt a new tactic. I would get a pillow slip, entice her into it and play through the protective material. She enjoyed this game greatly and would take part in variations of it every time I changed the bedclothes. Now, having learned a lot more about cats, I could have retrained her not to use her claws. Then, I did not know how.

Oddly enough, it was this kitten play aggression that won Ronnie's heart. She spent a lot of time ambushing him. She would hide behind the door and leap out at him, or balance on high furniture and leap down on him. He was lost in admiration of her courage.

'I can't believe that something as small as her would dare to attack me!' he exclaimed after wincing at yet another attack. One of her favourites was to leap off the bookcase on to his sleeping body. She used to aim at his groin, a sensitive area. Landing there never failed to wake him up fast.

As her fearlessness changed with the onset of a more sensible adult attitude to those larger than her, she stopped her attacks on him. By this time, he had had enough, too! Indeed, she became quite a timid little cat, disliking strangers, uncomfortable being picked up and refusing ever to get on a lap. She had inherited her mother's shy temperament.

She was completely relaxed, however, about travelling to and from our country cottage in Somerset. I had asked Professor Peter Neville, an expert on cat behaviour, about getting a cat who could tolerate car travel well, and he had advised me to get a kitten at eight weeks and drive her around in the car from this early age.

I had done what he said and taken Mog on short car drives from the first week that I adopted her. She therefore took the journey to and from Somerset to London entirely in her stride. She was equally at home in both territories, finding Somerset best for hunting and London best for idling under radiators. Accustoming her to car travel from as early an age as possible had been the way to make her feel safe in a car. What she learned in the first weeks of her life, being relaxed in the car and playing rough games with me, stayed with her forever.

When Mog was about 15 weeks old, I tried to leash train her. I didn't really know how to go about it and whenever the harness was put on her, she would slink around looking very unhappy. I didn't realize that I should have made sure that the harness was associated in her mind with food treats. If I had done this, perhaps she would have been able to tolerate it.

The other reason why I didn't persist in this was her fear of traffic. In London, our little house had a backyard alongside others, closed in by a block of flats at the end. The front door opened on to a street with traffic. Once I took her out into the front street – in my arms, but wearing a harness with the lead as a safety precaution. She was utterly terrified.

It dawned on me that I would be foolish to train her to tolerate traffic. She would be much safer if she remained terrified and just went out of the back door into the traffic-free gardens. There was a black and white cat down the end of the street who used to sit on his doorstep, stroll up the street and through the railings into the Westminster School playing fields at the top. One day he vanished. He had been run over by a speeding car. Although Mog was happy travelling inside a car, it was safer for her future if she remained frightened of them in the street.

During her first year living with us, my father died, not in hospital but at home. I visited him there for the last time, but was allowed just an hour at his bedside. My stepmother kept me out of the room where he lay. She wanted to make sure he did not know that he was dying. She feared I might tell him or that my visit might alert him to his true situation. Such is the denial and fear of death in our society.

He wouldn't have minded if I had mentioned it. He was very matter of fact about death, which I admired. He took it in his stride. About a year before his death, I had looked at the peeling wallpaper in his dining room and said, 'You must do something about that wallpaper, Daddy.'

'Shan't bother,' he said. 'I shall be dead soon, anyway. It will see me out.'

Fortunately, while I was there, my stepmother had to go to visit her mother, who was also ill. So I had a chance to sit by his bed for a little while.

'Do not be afraid of death,' Ronnie had told me before I visited. He had seen people die during his active service in the war. 'There is nothing frightening about dead people. You see the body and you see that the person is just not there.' But a day later, when my father died, I was not with him. My stepmother had him to herself.

There was no proper funeral. He had laid down in his will that his body was 'to be disposed of as cheaply as is consistent with human dignity'. Honouring his wishes meant we went to the crematorium and saw the coffin move off without a word of recollection or of mourning spoken. My stepmother, my brother, Ronnie and I walked in, sat down, watched the coffin depart and then walked out again.

The time after his death coincided with Mog's developing into a very skilful hunter. It was almost as if she had inherited my father's obsession with hunting. When he was a young man, he had hunted as much as he could afford. In middle age, he had hunted six days a week, following two separate packs of hounds in order to get that number of days. He would undoubtedly have gone out on Sundays, too, if he had found a hunt that did so. It is not an activity of which I can approve, either in men or cats, but I understand that cats cannot make a moral choice. They are hardwired in their brains to hunt.

In London, apart from one bedraggled pigeon, Mog caught nothing, maybe because there was nothing much to catch. In Somerset, she began to take a toll of the local mice. Rats she never dared attack and the rabbits that lived up the hill a full two fields away were too far out of her territory to be available as prey.

When we left our country cottage in Somerset for one in Oxfordshire one summer, she discovered pheasants. The local farmers ran a shoot and released hundreds of pheasants every year. These were kept in chicken runs for the first weeks of their lives and then allowed to roam where they wanted. They were completely unprepared for life in the wild. Most of them had probably never seen a cat.

Since they were used to humans feeding them regularly, they would cluster round our small house and spend hours in the garden, more like poultry than wild game. Mog was fascinated by them. For a whole summer, she would painstakingly stalk them until she was near enough to pounce. Then she would pause, reconsider, and saunter off as if the thought of pouncing had never occurred to her.

They were just too big for her. You could almost see a cartoon bubble above her head saying 'Better not!' What always made me laugh was her look of embarrassment. She would retreat with a kind of offended dignity, avoiding my eyes and clearly upset by my laughter.

She remained a small cat in body size but not so small, alas, round the tummy. In a word, she grew fat. Now I'd had one fat cat, Fat Ada, followed by another fat cat, Mog, and I also had a fat husband. 'Fat but fit' Ronnie insisted on calling himself. He was broad all round – not round like a ball with a huge waist size, but rather like a large tree trunk from shoulders to thighs.

'I am 18 stone of snarling muscle, not fat,' he would argue if I ever suggested a diet.

A fat cat and a fat husband had to be my fault, since I did the cooking. I started a healthy diet plan. We ate lots of green vegetables, wholemeal bread and pasta, no butter or cream, and not too much meat. I lost a little bit of weight as did Fat Mog. Ronnie lost none at all. I found out that he was simply increasing the size of his lunches and that, worse still, on the sly he was giving extra titbits to Mog! It was demoralizing. Slowly, butter, then meat, then cream came back into our meals, as I gave up the battle.

Mog, having been wary of all other cats, began to make a friend. A large black cat began appearing in the garden. His coat was always covered in dust, as if he slept somewhere dirty. I had met him first on the wall of a garden higher up the street. I happened to be carrying a small pork pie at the time, so I broke off a bit and put it on the wall for him. He ate it voraciously.

Five doors up the street, a neighbour asked me if I would like to come and see her kittens. She had neglected to get her new female cat spayed in time and the inevitable five kittens were, all of them, black. I resisted the temptation of taking one! The little black kittens looked as if Mog's new friend had been busy. He had also caused concern further up the street by breaking into the house and eating the resident cat's food.

Naturally, I fed him when I saw him nearby and soon he was coming to the garden regularly. He was wary of human contact, never coming close enough to be picked up. By now I knew enough to realize that he was a potential danger to Mog. Not only could she catch the fleas that dropped off him in the garden, but if they had a fight, she might become infected with FIV.

A proper fight was unlikely, because she seemed to have an almost flirtatious attitude towards him. She would sit at the open back door that summer, admiring him as he dozed on the paving stones. He clearly fascinated her and it seemed to me that she was a fan of his feline masculinity. She had been spayed, of course, but she still had the capacity to admire a really handsome tom. In return, he condescended to notice her, but she no longer had the *je ne sais quoi* to interest him.

I had to do something to keep her safe and to help him survive. Tomcats that are not neutered lead dangerous lives. They roam round the streets in search of un-neutered female cats, risking their lives in the traffic. They fight each other and break into houses in search of sex. They caterwaul loudly at night. Those who dislike cats often throw things at them. They do not live very long, as a result.

Castration would give this cat the best chance of survival, even if he continued to live on the street. Most castrated stray cats put on weight a few months after the snip. As their male hormones diminish, they settle down to a more sedate life, without fights, reducing the risk of being run over. For truly feral cats, neutering them and then putting them back on the street or farm where they live is probably the best way to improve their lives.

After about six weeks, during which I put the food bowl nearer and nearer to me, he came close enough for me to pick him up. I had put the tiniest amount of food in the bowl. When I lifted him, to my surprise he did not struggle very strongly and was easy to put in the cat carrier. I took him to the vet for castration and, at the same time, asked the vet to treat him for fleas and worms, and give him the first vaccination.

When I took him home, back to my garden, and let him out of the carrier, I was expecting him to rush out of it and disappear to wherever he had his dusty hidey hole. Instead, he walked out and immediately got stuck into the bowl of food I had put out for him. Black Cat, as I was now unimaginatively calling him, wasn't a feral and he was very hungry, having missed his breakfast in preparation for the anaesthetic.

So now I had two cats – a cat who lived indoors and a cat who lived somewhere else, but spent a lot of time in my garden. I cut a cat flap into the outside backyard lavatory, a relic of Victorian days no longer used as a lavatory but now useful as a cat shelter. At weekends when we were in the country, I left a bowl of food and one of water for him inside the outhouse, and installed a bed. Black Cat put on weight and lost most of the dust that clung to his fur, but he still kept a little distance away from me. Perhaps he remembered that the last time I had handled him, he had lost his tomhood!

It seemed to me he might never make a proper house cat. He was so jumpy and nervous. Then one day when I was sitting on a chair in the backyard, he jumped up onto my lap, purring loudly. It was a complete turnaround, from fear and caution to love. I have seen this extraordinary change from fear to confidence in other cats and it always fills me with amazed delight.

Black Cat had been a would-be lap cat all along, more of a lap cat than Mog, once his fear had diminished. I took him for his second vaccination, and a test, now available for the first time, showed that he did not have FIV.

But Black Cat had lost his glamour for Mog. She no longer gave him admiring glances, or sat demurely while he strutted past. Instead, she made it clear that, robbed of his masculinity by castration, he had no place in her life. Perhaps his allure for her had been his strong male scent, now diminished by the snip. Cats identify friend and foe by scent, and perhaps a strong male scent, like aftershave, remains attractive even to a neutered female.

Certainly, he was altered for the worse in her eyes and perhaps in her nose, too. And, despite being unavailable for feline sex, she didn't like this new metro asexual male. Black Cat was now a turn-off, not a turn-on. Anyway, I felt I couldn't take him into my home, which is where he wanted to be. He would sit outside the back door with a yearning look on his face.

Luckily, my nephew was in need of a cat. He didn't know he needed one, of course, but when I asked him to look after Black Cat while we were away on holiday for a month, he agreed. I knew that his favourite book, as a child, had been *The Outside Cat,* the story of a cat who longed to become an indoor cat.

He would be a sucker for what I planned! By the end of the month, he had renamed the black cat Mac and agreed with me that he needed this cat to make his life complete. Mac lived happily ever after for a full lifespan, thanks to a bit of unfair aunt manipulation by me!

Mog was happier without him and Ronnie wasn't emotionally ready for a second cat. Fat Ada and now Fat Mog had trained him into a state of mind where he had grown to love them both, but he was not yet a fully committed cat lover, ready to fall in love with any furry creature with a wavy tail. He now loved particular cats, but not all cats. There was room for further improvement in his attitude to felines!

His lifestyle was still not that of a cat owner. Although he was still jetting off to trouble spots, the trouble spots themselves had changed. It was the time of hijacks. Terrorists had discovered that they could get international attention for their cause by taking over a plane. Not all hijacks ended in the death of passengers, as most of the terrorists in those days weren't particularly keen on committing suicide. Terrorism was still primarily political, not religious.

Ronnie and his friend Chris Dobson, having been sent to and reported on a couple of hijacks, had started working on their first book about terrorism, *The Carlos Complex*. Later, various American academics piled into the subject and made it their own, but at the beginning Ronnie was one of the first experts in that field.

Writing books meant he spent more time at home in between foreign trips and he had more time for daily cat care. So when my mother was diagnosed with cancer, I was able to spend about three days of every week with her. During my absence, Mog slept on the bed with Ronnie and probably shared many of his meals – he enjoyed feeding her off his fork. My absence was bad for her figure!

My mother's illness taught me to accept death, in all its awesome power. Accepting death is not something that our society does well. Once most people died in their own homes, often visited by their friends to say goodbye. Now they die hidden away in hospitals, nursing homes or, if they are lucky, hospices. As for me, I had an unthinking optimism about medicine's power to soothe.

Her death was a shock, an unpleasant insight into the way we die now. She had been admitted to a nursing home on St Valentine's day, after a fall. Officially, her disease was squamous cell carcinoma of the tongue. After a week in the nursing home, the nurses told me she was not going to get better. Probably the cancer had spread to some inner organ, maybe the pancreas. Tests to find out would simply distress a dying 80 year old.

My mother refused to admit that her cancer was terminal, and would not have anything to do with the local hospice. So she died inch by inch, moment by moment, organ by organ, over seven days and four hours from the moment she stopped drinking liquid. For me, by her bedside, these were the worst days of my life so far. Nothing in all my previous years of life had prepared me for this death – the length of the process and the mixture of agony in my vigil.

My brother and I sat by her bed day and night, listening to her breathing, waiting for the end. Sometimes Candy, the tortoiseshell nursing-home cat, joined us in our death watch, sitting at the end of the bed, alternately purring or sleeping, eyes opening to blink then closing again. She had been a great comfort to my mother, while she was still conscious. Now a cat's presence was a comfort to my brother and me.

My mother's eyes were sinking back into the cavities of the skull beneath the skin. Her cheeks, already sunken because her false teeth were not in, fell ever further inwards. Her nose was sharpening – 'sharp as a pen' is how Shakespeare describes it. Slowly, the individual features that made her my mother were being taken over by something more impersonal.

The skin on her face became first white, then as the days succeeded each other, changed to parchment yellow. There were red blotches on her cheeks and dull red stains in the inner hollow of her eyes.

There was no easy transition from life to death. She had refused to drink, so she could not take painkillers. I went off to fetch a morphine pump for her but there was a delay in getting the morphine itself. With difficulty, I coaxed her into drinking two dissolved painkillers through a straw. For the past year I had coaxed and bullied her into eating and drinking so often that, luckily, she would do for me what she would not do for the nurses.

What I didn't know was that she was being put on the Liverpool Care Pathway, a method by which food and drink are withdrawn from somebody in order to help them die. The Liverpool Care Pathway, alas, causes suffering of its own.

The nursing home told me not to offer her any more water and I was afraid to do so in case she choked on it. I should have taken no notice of their instructions. I should not have deferred to the doctors and nurses.

As I sat by her, the morphine pump would make occasional buzzes. These, it turned out, occurred as another shot of narcotic was delivered into her body. I did not know this and some of the nurses were unfamiliar with a pump, too. So I reported these buzzes and wondered if the pump was working properly.

She was also having subsidiary injections of some kind of painkiller, perhaps because the morphine pump was not reliable. These would last for about four hours during which time she would sleep. When they wore off, she would resurface into consciousness.

Her words were indistinguishable, although once she joined in when I was singing her a lullaby, as I tried to help her go back to sleep. To some visitors, she smiled. To me, she seemed to implore.

Her mouth was now drying and she would try to moisten her lips. Her tongue had swollen and pieces of dry skin peeled off it. There was a great grey mouth ulcer on the inside of her cheek. I tried to moisten her lips with a mixture of cider and lemon juice, using a little brush sold to me by the local chemist. But I applied too much liquid and she began to choke.

All I could think about was that I desperately wanted my mother to die, to be out of her suffering. I could perhaps have ended it by deliberately making her choke. Yet I could not bring myself to kill her in this way. I stopped putting on the liquid, but seeing her suffering from thirst was agonizing. I blame myself for letting doctors and nurses take control of her dying. I should have been able to help her in some way.

Every four hours the nurses moved her, to take the pressure off her already sore body. At these moments, I left the room but I could hear her saying to them, 'Don't hurt me,' and, 'I can't go on.' I could also see her distress each time she had to pee in the bed. I would lean over her and say, 'It's all right to do it here, Mum,' but she would look anxious and move her thin-stick arms about as if she was desperately trying to get out of bed. The prohibition against peeing in the wrong place goes right back to the first months of life; even dying did not diminish its force.

I had to ask for another painkilling injection for her. On one occasion, the nurse said, 'As soon as I can, I will do it' – a reasonable reply for her, but not for me. My brother bore our mother's distress better than I did. He felt that she was not in physical pain even though she was unhappy.

I did not agree. I would not have let any cat or any dog of mine continue this slow painful descent towards death. Luckily for them, euthanasia is available from any vet, but doctors do not have the freedom to mercy kill, like vets do. Whatever the Liverpool Care Pathway was meant to do, the 'Care' part of its name did not work well.

The horror of her passage from life to death was terrible to me. By now, her tortured body was seriously dehydrated. Her eyelashes were crusted with what she had once called 'sleepy dust' – nursery talk to make her children smile. When she opened the lids, they would lift up slowly. They were gluey and sticky with drying tears.

By now she had been three days without liquid. Her frail, aged body should have died. It didn't. Her 'weak' heart beat steadily on. Her temperature rose – probably the sign of a urinary infection. The doctor agreed not to treat it, to hasten the end. But I had been asking for her life not to be prolonged, when I should have been asking for her last days to be made comfortable. Without the antibiotics her body was red hot.

All that day she was Cheyne-Stokes breathing. This is a kind of respiration when a strong breath is followed by a series of smaller breaths until it looks as if breathing has stopped. Just at this moment of silence, a large breath recurs. Her throat began to rattle – a death rattle, we thought, and my brother made arrangements to stay another 24 hours.

On Tuesday she grew even hotter, probably with pneumonia. Her body would be shaken by occasional spasms, like the ones that occur just before sleep when you think you are falling. Her lungs began to sound noisy. Sometimes, the intake of her breath would sound like a groan, but it was an involuntary noise.

One nurse told me not to leave her, even for ten minutes. Death could be any time, she said. But death did not come. The chaplain administered extreme unction. Her local vicar visited and prayed, as did another very special friend. Yet a third vicar, in his 80s and partially blind, took a bus across Oxford two or three times a day to sit by her and give me time off. He would sit there reading the psalms in the authorized language.

I have laughed at Church of England vicars many times. I have enjoyed the silliness of vicars in Barbara Pym novels. But I had now found a time and a place when I needed them. Unlike ordinary visitors, who came and went away shaken, fearful and often crying, these specialists were imperturbable in their compassion. They took death, and life after it, for granted.

On Wednesday, a little miracle happened. One of my mother's hands lay outside the coverings. It was bluish in colour. I took hold of it and as I did so, it grasped back. By now, her face was even more ghastly, her eyes were firmly closed, and there was no sign that she was conscious. Yet she was definitely holding my hand.

I felt a great joy. We stayed like this for six hours. I talked to her. I told her of my love. I told her how happiness awaited her. I believed she could hear me. Her hand turned from blue to pink and she did not die. I did not mean to delay her passing, just the reverse, but perhaps I had unwittingly strengthened her link to life.

By Thursday, my brother had to go back to work but my mother was still alive. Just. Her breath no longer rattled and her breathing was shallower. Nurses came in to admire her tenacity. To my great pleasure, Candy the hospital cat joined her on the bed again. The doctor stopped giving any forecasts of when she would die. She should have been dead three days ago. Without Candy's comforting presence I do not know if I could have continued my vigil.

For another 24 hours I stayed there, waiting. I sang hymns occasionally, as much for my comfort as for hers. She gave no sign of listening to them. Only the occasional twitch, in response to talk by me or others, made me think that nonetheless perhaps she still heard us.

Thursday dragged on. At eight o'clock that night, something changed. I do not know what it was. Her breathing and her body seemed much the same, but by now I was so tuned in to the strange language of her dying that I must have picked up some alteration in tone.

I walked over to her and picked up her hand. It was cold to the wrist. Dead cold. Quite different from the cold of the living hand that had held me as a baby. A passing nurse took her blood pressure and told me it was dropping. I sang her a hymn. I told her how much I loved her. I sang the old lullaby of my childhood, 'Golden Slumbers Kiss Your Eyes'. One long intake of breath and she stopped breathing for ever.

I had failed my mother when she most needed my help. I walked out of the nursing home and let them organize the disposal of the body. It was not my mother any more.

I swore I would not let anyone else I love have that kind of death.

Chapter 6

William and George

William was the cat who really turned Ronnie around, completing his conversion to felines. Those who hate cats might think Ronnie had turned to the dark side, but I prefer to see it as a turn to joy and light. He changed from a man who wasn't interested in cats into a man who learned to love two individual cats, first Ada then Mog, then into a man who was entranced with a cat.

They say that you can never change a man. They warn you not to marry in the hope of doing so. Well, I did not change Ronnie, but my cats did, and William was the cat who finalized the process. After William, Ronnie was a fully paid-up member of the real-men-who-love-cats brigade. Strong, brave men can love cats, too!

It was William's grace and beauty that did the trick. Tabby and white William was a really glamorous cat, with long hair and exquisite golden eyes edged with black, as if he was wearing eyeliner.

He had come from a cat hoarder's household and had grown up with exceptionally good social skills towards other cats. As a tiny kitten, when he was brought home to us, he was ready to make friends with Little Mog. She hated this idea. She didn't want a friend.

Carefully, I installed William in a crate in the main room, so that Mog could come and go, taking a look at him when she chose. She chose to ignore him altogether and took up residence upstairs as far away from the crate as possible. She spent the first five days simply sitting on one of the spare-room beds, refusing to acknowledge the presence of this kitten intruder. At night, he remained downstairs so that Mog could sleep undisturbed in my bed. For the first night of his stay, she refused to join me – the first time she had ever missed crawling into bed with me.

I didn't really understand her response, because I knew so little about cats at this point. I had thought she would welcome a new friend, or at least welcome a tiny, appealing kitten. One of the next-door cats, a tabby female, Winchester, had welcomed a new kitten, and started grooming it within an hour of its arrival. I hoped Mog would mother the new arrival.

No such chance. She made it clear that she was stressed, unhappy and in a mega feline sulk. Her response made me understand two things – that cats have individual personalities and that I knew next to nothing about the species. I didn't even know how to introduce her to William using scent swapping (so that he smelled of the family scent rather than a strange scent) so I had stressed her out more than was necessary.

She never much liked him. Like most cats, she worked out a way to live with him, ignoring him as much as possible, keeping out of his way, and using separate beds. I hadn't even realized that I should put down food in two separate locations, so that they could avoid each other while eating. But Mog shared the food bowl, using it when he didn't – this worked because I was feeding *ad lib* so they could come and snack at any time.

Theoretically speaking, cats can regulate their food intake. Most of my cats have not understood that this theory applied to them. Mog in particular failed to self-regulate. As she grew older (she was eight when William arrived) she got greedier and greedier, putting on an impressive amount of weight. Personally, I think this was an inherited problem, as her mother Eronwy was a small, fat cat, like a furry version of a short Welsh woman who had eaten too much bara brith.

Ad lib feeding had to stop. I changed Mog to a diet food and tried to feed the two cats separately. She never actually lost weight but the diet food may have stopped her from getting obese. However, it didn't have a good effect on her character. From that time onwards, she lived for food.

William, who wasn't very turned on by food, continued to have other interests, such as hunting mice, rabbits and even weasels. Mog began to lose interest in hunting mice, directing her efforts towards stealing food instead. Ronnie, a man who loved his food and was much the same shape as her, could not be relied upon not to give her titbits from his plate and I was a bit lax in remembering to keep her totally separate from William's dish.

I hope it wasn't because of this lack of food discipline at home that she developed a bladder stone. Mog's stone was diagnosed the week after I had decided to cancel my pet insurance. Luckily for me, I had forgotten to do so. The insurance was still in place. My forgetfulness had come to my aid. Mog had the kind of bladder stone that needs to be removed by an operation, not the kind that can be dissolved by a prescription diet. The fee for her operation (by a London vet) was over one thousand pounds and she was put on a special diet for life.

The new diet came in tins and smelled quite disgusting. At first (after I had mixed it with an ordinary tin and slowly increased the proportions in favour of the new food) she ate it. Then something unfortunate happened. I found a half eaten corpse of a bird in the garden. Simultaneously, Mog had severe stomach trouble.

That meant another visit to the vet (unfortunately, not part of the previous treatment paid for by the insurer), who suggested she had eaten something that had given her food poisoning, the bird, probably. Mog's response was extraordinary. Faced with the new special tinned food, she absolutely refused to eat the tiniest speck of it. She was reacting according to an instinct we all have, cats and even humans. If we are sick after eating a certain food, we decide that's what made us ill, and most of us will never touch it again. Mog decided that the cause of her tummy upset was cat food, not the bird, and she wouldn't eat it.

Indeed, it was worse than that. She wouldn't eat any food at all. I sped to the vet and got a dry version of the prescription food. She would eat about two little biscuits of this before refusing to eat any more. For 24 hours I hand fed her two little biscuits every 20 minutes. The following day, she increased her appetite to four biscuits at a time and I could feed her every half an hour. On the third day she was eating normally again. And, more importantly, she was eating the special food that would protect her from bladder stones in the future.

While she was becoming an old lady, William was flourishing. He had had a bad start, a repository for almost every parasite known to vets, thanks to his upbringing in a household with 54 other cats. But that overcrowded upbringing had taught him a skill that most cats do not have. He never responded to Mog's hostility with hostility of his own.

He even held his own with a neighbouring cat, Gizmo, who had taken to beating up all the cats in the locality, including poor fat Little Mog. Gizmo was what cat experts call a despot cat. He attacked without mercy. After several abscesses in her tail area, due to his biting her as she fled from him, Mog refused to go out without being bodyguarded by me. There were no microchip cat flaps in those days and Gizmo would have come into the house if I'd had an ordinary cat flap. So I had to let both cats in and out by the back door.

William, despite being a very gentle cat, was able to cope with Gizmo. When Gizmo prepared to attack him, William would never run. He just flopped on to his side with all his claws at the ready for defence. This move may also have had elements of submissiveness about it, giving Gizmo the message that 'I am too small a cat to attack' as well as the other message, which was 'I have every single claw ready to scratch you if you attack.' We don't really know enough about cat body language to be sure which message predominates!

Gizmo, however, got the message, or perhaps both messages, and after a bit of posturing – walking stiff legged with bushy tail, side on to the recumbent William – he would walk away. The secret of William's success was that he never ran.

After waiting for a while to make sure Gizmo wouldn't be coming back, William would rise to his feet and get on with his life. This included entering Gizmo's house and eating Gizmo's food. I had thought William was nice but dim until I saw him surreptitiously eating Gizmo's food when I was visiting my neighbours next door. He had quietly entered via the cat flap, and I realized he had a natural sneakiness and rat-like cunning that allowed him to get what he wanted without getting hurt. These are the qualities that make for a good journalist, and Ronnie's love affair with William was enhanced by seeing these journalistic traits displayed to such a good end.

The only time William did display hostility was towards vets. He loathed, simply loathed, having his temperature taken up the backside. Once, when he had eaten about a hundred cat vitamin pills after cleverly pushing the container off the kitchen table, I had to rush him to the vet in case he was poisoned. As she stuck the thermometer into his body, he turned smartly round and bit her hard. 'He can't be that ill,' she remarked, nursing her hand. From that time on I had to warn vets about his hostility to this particular demeaning veterinary technique. None of my cats have enjoyed having their temperature taken, most have flinched, but William was the only one who bit.

He bit me once and that was when I unwittingly hurt him as I picked him up. After biting, he purred and licked me in apology. It turned out that he had an abscess that must have developed from a bite, perhaps by a rat, or more likely Gizmo had caught him unawares. I am pleased to say that it was an abscess on the front of his body, showing that (unlike Mog whose abscesses were always on the backside) he had faced his foe without running away. He had the gentleness that came from confidence and strength.

Mog eventually accepted him as a member of her family, although by no means her favourite member. I was her favourite and after me, Ronnie. William came last – tolerated rather than loved.

Mog's next illness occurred when she lost interest in food. As food was very important in her life, when she started eating just a little, I thought this required a visit to the vet. I had also noticed that she gave a kind of yelp each time she jumped down from the bed, as though she was in pain. Cats rarely cry out in pain, so I reckoned this must be serious.

'What do you think is wrong,' I asked anxiously as the vet put Mog on the floor and watched her gait. To his expert eye, Mog wasn't walking comfortably. Cats rarely limp but she wasn't walking with ease.

'We will have to X-ray her.'

That X-ray showed she was suffering from severe arthritis, so she was prescribed a painkiller. This brought back her appetite, showing that her failure to eat was because she was in constant pain. She also regained more interest in life, spending less time on the bed and going out a little bit more, when bodyguarded by me.

My immediate reaction was to feel guilty. In her early years I had fed her quite a lot of human food – raw chicken, little bits of steak. I wondered if her diet in the first year of her life had meant that she had not had the nourishment she needed for bone growth. Could this have predisposed her to arthritis? From that moment on I have been careful about feeding kittens a proper complete cat food, without too many extras or treats. Home diets are just too complicated for ordinary non-experts to get right.

I set about turning our house into a home for a disabled feline. My first purchase was a heated pad for cats, which was inside a sort of metal tube. It looked rather like a torpedo with an entrance. This extraordinary device, which is no longer sold, allowed her to sleep warm and secure, undisturbed by William during the night. I also put a covered stool near my bed so that she could jump up and down in small steps, but as she grew older, she favoured the tube over the inside of the bed.

I bought two cat ramps. One led to the sofa, where I put an extra soft cat bed made out of an old duvet covered with material. The other ramp led to my desk. On the desk was another cat bed without the tube but with an electrically warmed bottom covered with a fleece. She dozed there happily while I worked at my computer. There was an advantage to me, as she no longer interfered with my typing, preferring to stay warm.

Before she became so arthritic, she had enjoyed basking in the sunlight on the windowsill of the living room. Having already put a ramp to the sofa, it seemed a bit much to buy a third ramp. The house was filling up with disabled feline equipment. So I contented myself with another covered stool in front of an armchair, which I moved near the window. Now she could reach the sill in a series of small jumps.

The litter trays (I had one per cat) needed a bit of alteration, too. Disabled humans need a higher lavatory seat; disabled cats need the opposite, a lower tray. Mog could still get into hers, but she found difficulty turning round within it. So I got rid of the litter-tray cover.

'This house has become a cat hospital,' remarked Ronnie one day, surveying the living room.

He had a point. The mantelpiece had become the feline pharmacy, the place to keep a tube of feline constipation remedy and a small container of liquid painkiller. There was the ramp up to the sofa, which was itself half covered with a very large, soft cat bed. There was the cushioned stool leading to the armchair leading to the windowsill with yet another soft cat bed. One of the occasional tables was the place for a soft brush, a harder brush and a comb to groom the areas of her body that Mog could no longer twist to reach.

It was these living arrangements which Ronnie found so funny that inspired his book *One Hundred Ways to Live with a Cat Addict*, which was entirely based on me! This was very much a change from his normal books about terrorism, and it caused him some irritation to find that it sold as well as, if not better than, the serious volumes.

I laughed with him at the time, but the memory makes me tearful now. About ten years later, the whole house was to become a husband hospital with chair lift, zimmer frames upstairs and downstairs, a special armchair that helped him get up, and even a special hospital bed. By then he was living in constant pain, like Mog had been, which even with painkillers was difficult for him to bear.

For Mog, as for him, the disability aids – the ramps, heated beds and painkillers – gave her three more years of decent life. She became very close to me, only happy if she was in the same room. She would move from room to room, following me despite the pain and effort this required.

Then she stopped eating for the third and last time.

'I'm afraid it's kidney disease,' was the vet's verdict. 'If you can leave her with us for 48 hours, we can flush out her kidneys with a drip and that might give her three months more.'

'Could you put in the drip, so that I could take her home and keep her on it at home for that 48 hours?' I asked.

Little Mog, now aged 13, had lately become almost completely deaf and was therefore anxious about being anywhere but at home. She was so dependent on me that she liked to keep me in her sight at all times. I did not want to put her through 48 hours in a veterinary clinic with its frightening associations, strange smells and the scent of nearby dogs.

'I don't think I want to put her through anything more,' I told the vet. 'Let's do it now.'

This time I had got it right. I could not explain any treatment to her. Any veterinary procedure would be an ordeal without her understanding its reason. I had begun, also, to accept the fact that all cats and all people have to die. What matters is the how not the why. I held Little Mog as she crossed the river from life to death, to that place where there is no sorrow or crying nor any more pain.

Both Ronnie and I missed her dreadfully. As with Fat Ada, I kept thinking I saw her just on the edges of my sight. I also thought I heard her step on the stairs. In a way, this was a comfort for me, the feeling that perhaps she had not entirely left us. Perhaps her spirit stayed with us. We were lucky we had William still.

By now, I was involved in my local cat rescue, and I knew how desperately homes were needed for unwanted cats and kittens. I had little hesitation, therefore, in deciding I wanted another cat, preferably a kitten so that William could more easily bond with it. I thought that it would perhaps work out better if I got another female, not a male. Indeed, by then that suggestion was on my website. I didn't follow my own advice. An eagerness to add another cat triumphed over good sense.

George was the new addition to the family. He had been rescued with his littermates from a barn, his mother having abandoned them. George had therefore been hand-reared with a bottle. He was small, black and very, very funny.

His early life on the bottle meant that he adored humans. All of them. When the gas central-heating man came to do a boiler inspection, George inspected the boiler with him. He sat close, staring at the boiler with a considered air, as if he himself could tell what needed testing or replacing. It was almost as if he imitated us humans. It is possible that he thought he *was* human.

He was also fearless. As a small kitten he jumped on to the lavatory seat, staggered wildly and then fell in. Luckily, I was at hand to fish him out, and from then on the seat had to be closed for his safety. He was fascinated by the rush of water when the lavatory was flushed. He also enjoyed playing with water when it gushed from the kitchen tap.

When he was a little older, he fell into the icy garden pond, fortunately, again, at a time when I was there to haul him out with the pond net. Then he jumped into it deliberately just to see what would happen this time, and I let him swim to the side to get out. Once again, he jumped in and, perhaps sensing that he no longer had my complete attention by this daring move (as by now I knew he could swim), he never bothered to do it again.

He liked puddles, too. He would deliberately wade into

them, looking at his own reflection, or stir up the water with his paw, or even trail his tail so that it fell into the water. Mud was interesting to him. He enjoyed walking in mud patches and then jumping on Ronnie's lap. The resulting shout of, 'Get that bloody cat off me,' didn't frighten him at all. For him, it was part of the fun.

He ran up the large oak tree in our garden. As a kitten, William had done the same. He had got to the first branch and then walked along it to the slender end until it buckled under his weight. He had clung helplessly for a few seconds and then, with a kitten cry of alarm, fallen to the ground, landing unhurt.

George was more adventurous. He didn't stop at the first branch, but climbed higher and higher until he was about 25 feet up, and he didn't seem at all worried. The worries were mine. It was a freezing cold day and I didn't dare wait to see if he could come down of his own accord.

'Georgie, Georgie,' I called. He gazed happily down at me as if to say, 'Look at me!' and then climbed a few branches higher – just to show me what he could do. Neither I (because of a fear of heights) nor Ronnie (who was now in his 80s) could climb up after him.

After about half an hour of rattling the food dishes and the dried-food container in vain, I was beginning to despair. Then I heard a tractor passing by along the cart track that leads to our home. I waved it down.

'Can you please help with my cat?' I asked.

'What's up?' the driver asked, climbing down from his tractor.

'My kitten is up the oak tree and he won't come down.'

The tractor driver (may the Big Cat in the sky reward him) volunteered to rescue George. He climbed up 25 feet and climbed down using just one hand, no mean feat, holding George in the other. George didn't struggle. He was completely without anxiety about this experience. He just sauntered off with a self-satisfied air, while I thanked the brave tractor driver effusively.

Ronnie's walking stick slightly worried William but George liked to play with it. He would run on ahead, then turn and rush back, skidding between Ronnie and the walking stick. He leaped on to gates in order to be petted as we opened them. He jumped into the car and investigated it. He was happy to be cuddled by the postwoman. I had handed him to several people in the first four weeks after his arrival. He was so socialized to humans that he loved them all and had no fear.

I had perhaps gone from one extreme to another. From letting Little Mog play rough games and not giving her enough handling, I had made George into a complete human-centred softie. While Ronnie still preferred the utterly beautiful tabby and white William with his golden eyes and dark rims, I fell in love with sleek, all-black George.

He was full of fun. I was a keen gardener and used to put out cloches for early vegetables. George soon discovered these and would worm his way into them, looking at me to see my reaction as he sat upon the newly planted vegetables. When I laughed, he had achieved his aim.

He loved getting my attention. If I threw a catnip mouse on to the lawn, he would play with it, batting it about, throwing it up in the air, making enormous leaps into the air, twisting his body before landing again on the lawn. Sometimes he would lie on his side with the toy mouse in his front paws, then rake it with his back paws.

All this was done to make me laugh. If I stopped looking at him, he would stop playing with the toy mouse. If I continued and, better still, laughed out loud, he would redouble his efforts. He enjoyed poking the mouse into strange places, such as a rabbit hole, or the gaps between the slats of a garden seat, or even the gap at the bottom of the garden table's central leg. Then he would roll on his back and try to poke it out again while remaining upside down.

As he grew older, George began to bully William. He was aggressive to other cats. This was probably because as a bottle-fed kitten, he thought he was a human. If so, he thought he was a human that hated cats. William began to wear a cautious look. There wasn't blood on the carpet but there were standoffs. William, who was smaller and gentler, developed feline idiopathic cystitis, a stress-related disease.

By now, I was so fully in love with George that I couldn't bear to rehome him and, besides, Ronnie would not have stood for it. I did my best to help the cats lead separate lives. I put out two feeding locations and I shut George into a bedroom at night so that William could have the house to himself without worrying about George's presence. I was so bonded with George by then that sometimes I would sneak out of Ronnie's bed in the early hours and join George in the spare bedroom.

George had started serious hunting. Unfortunately, his first successful hunting episode was when he caught a greenfinch. If his first prey had been a mouse, I believe he would have concentrated on small mammals, but, alas, it was birds, and he became a specialist bird hunter. No winged being was safe from him – greenfinches, robins, blackbirds, partridges, and even once a very large, slow-moving pheasant.

I would come home to find feathers all over the garden and sometimes all over the kitchen. It was horrible. There wasn't much I could do to stop him without making him into an indoor-only cat. I tried to let him out after dawn and take him back indoors before dusk, so that ground-eating birds would be safe from him at these times. I put scrumpled up wire netting under the shrubs where he used to sit in order to ambush blackbirds.

When he could no longer conceal himself in the shrubs, he started taking an interest in rabbits. At the time, we had a huge colony of them. George started with baby rabbits and then graduated to young adults. Sometimes, he caught and killed one that was so large he could drag it home only with the greatest difficulty.

I love birds and I am particularly fond of rabbits. Each time I saw him dragging back a big bunny, pausing to get his breath, then dragging it again, I would feel guilty. How could I love this serial killer? How could I let him wreak destruction on wildlife? Worse still, why did I feel a kind of perverse pride in the hunting exploits of my mini black panther?

On a diet of cat food mixed with raw rabbit, George grew bigger, sleeker, more powerful and more fearless. I would feed the cats in the early evening, calling them in from the garden, and locking the cat flap at night. William would come in obediently. George began staying out later and later. He didn't need the food. He was going to catch his own evening meal.

He would arrive back at about 3am, waking me up as he jumped on the bed, whiskers quivering with the excitement of a night out in the moonlight. Where he had been and what he had been doing, I had no idea. Like an anxious wife pursuing an errant husband, I would go calling for him in the dark. He rarely came back, perhaps because by now he was more than three fields away hunting the hedgerows.

Then one evening he did not come back at all.

I slept poorly, waiting for the sound of the cat flap banging as he came in from the shadows of the dark garden. It never came, so at 4am, I got up, put on my shoes and coat and walked up and down the cart track, calling his name and lighting up the hedges with my torch. There was no responding flash of cat's eyes as I passed. There was no George.

I went back to bed and slept fitfully till the morning. Still no George. While he had sometimes been out very late in the autumn night, he had always been home well before breakfast.

He had disappeared.

For the next week I walked alongside every roadside hedge, hunting for him, hoping to find him lying wounded by a car, or hoping, perhaps, just to find his body so that I need not torture myself with the thought of him dying slowly without my help. I must have walked about 25 miles. I walked the fields and into the little copse nearby, calling and calling his name.

I put up handmade posters on the nearby village noticeboards and lampposts. I distributed them to local vets. I checked the local lost and found websites and made door-to-door inquiries at the nearest hamlet. When the postman told me he had seen a black cat in the nearby village, I tracked the cat to some local stables. 'We've had him for four years,' they told me.

I was so determined to get George back that I could hardly believe them. The cat looked like George, but then so did every black cat in the neighbourhood. I considered kidnapping some of the local black toms and taking them somewhere where I could check for George's microchip. Then I realized that not only would I be in trouble with the owners, but that I would be causing similar distress to them as I was feeling.

The pain of having a cat put down was nothing compared with the pain of not knowing what had happened to George. Until then, I had not understood the need we humans have for closure, for knowing the outcome of a tragedy. Now I knew.

The uncertainty of his fate literally gave me nightmares. I would dream that I saw him in a gamekeeper's snare; or that he was slowly crawling down our cart track, dragging his legs, which had been paralysed by a traffic accident; or that he was shut up in somebody's barn, slowly dying of dehydration.

'I can't bear not knowing,' I said to Ronnie, who enfolded me in one of his bear hugs, and cried. My big brave husband was crying for a cat.

Wiliam seemed upset, too. He became extra cautious, peering in through the cat flap before coming in, walking round the shrubs in the garden, sniffing with extra care, spraying at key points in the shrubbery – something he had never done before.

'I think he misses George,' said Ronnie.

'I'm not so sure. He may just be making sure that George isn't hiding, ready to ambush him,' I replied.

After about a month, it was clear I was right. Far from missing George, William was only too happy that he had disappeared. He began to wear a more jaunty look. Now he would roll on the carpet at our feet in the living room, rather than jump up and sit on the windowsill. He started sharing our bed. He 'came out of himself' as the old phrase goes. Relaxed confidence took the place of his previous caution. For the first time in his life he was an only cat – and he loved every moment.

He particularly loved being photographed. If a photographer turned up to take my photo for an article or for the back of a book jacket, William didn't need coaxing to be part of the shot. He would walk into it.

I particularly remember a time when I gave an interview about cats to a small TV company. They sent a man with a camera, who did both filming and interviewing. It wasn't a success. The interviewer/cameraman gave up shooting me altogether and simply concentrated on William, who sat and rolled and walked right up to the camera, glorying in being the star. I never saw what happened to the resulting film. If it was used at all, it was footage of a glamorous tabby and white cat with a voice over by a far less glamorous human female, me.

Ronnie recovered more quickly from the loss of George than I did. He had always had a decided preference for William over any other cat, although George had made him laugh.

Ronnie was now slightly unsteady on his feet, and George's determination to make a game of weaving between his legs and his walking stick had been a worry for him. William, an older cat, was more sedate and I would see them walking along the cart track together at a slow pace that suited them both. William would occasionally linger behind to investigate something in the hedge, then run to catch up Ronnie.

William's last few months of life seemed to take place in a series of sunsets that edged his fur with golden light and echoed the gold of his eyes. I would do anything to see them both again, walking back up the track towards me with the setting sun behind them.

Chapter 7

Friendship is stronger than death

William's grace and beauty had changed Ronnie into a proper cat lover. So great was the transformation that once, when he was suffering from hallucinations due to morphine, he looked down and saw a small silver kitten on the floor.

'I'm not having kittens, I'm seeing them,' he said.

'You have finally become a cat addict like me,' I joked.

'You've taken me over,' he replied. But in reality it was William, not me, who deserved the credit. His beauty had transformed Ronnie's attitude to cats in a way that I could never have achieved. William had seduced him utterly.

After William, we had a few months with only a foster cat, Boomer, and then some time without a cat altogether. In 2010 I adopted Tilly, a little, dark brown tortoiseshell cat who had stayed unwanted in the local cat shelter for 18 months. From a terrified animal she had become extremely loving to me. She was fond of Ronnie, too, but not excessively so.

I think Ronnie felt a little bit left out of our relationship. 'If I hear you saying something in a really loving tone of voice,' he once said, 'I know you're talking to Tilly rather than me.' Tilly was helping me to keep going as I recovered from breast cancer and cared for Ronnie with his two different cancers.

I had help, of course, every day. A stream of people from an agency would visit Ronnie each morning at 7am and help him wash and dress. At first they were able to guide him up by the stair lift to the shower on the first floor. Then, as he grew too weak to be safe in the shower (even on a little chair), they would wash him thoroughly from head to toe on the side of his bed.

They were gentle and caring – Carol, Mary, Ewa, Gabrjela, Georgie and others. I grew to admire their unfailing kindness, as well as their efficiency. Being a carer is not highly paid but they did their work with courtesy, and some of what they had to do was very disagreeable. Their kindness was an inspiration to me, then and now. I think, indeed I know, they liked Ronnie a lot. I would hear him telling them stories of his life as a war reporter.

True, we never knew which of them would turn up, but as we liked all of them, that hardly mattered. 'It's nice to have a new person,' said Ronnie with his usual optimism. 'I can bore them with all my old stories.'

As well as the carers' team, there were regular visits from community nurses. Ever since Ronnie had developed an ulcer on his leg, they had come two or three times a week. When the ulcer waned, it was twice a week. When the ulcer got larger, it was three times a week. It waxed and waned like the moon for more than two years, possibly reflecting the state of his immune system. The nurses taught me how to bandage it up, so at moments of crisis or on bank holidays, I could do it without them.

They almost all had cats. Morse and Lewis, beautiful indoor Burmese brothers, named after the TV series, belonged to Helen. It was Morse who proved to me that cats are ragingly individual. Lewis died of old age and Morse was left on his own.

'We're going to get a kitten,' said Helen.

'He might not want a kitten,' I warned her. 'Cats aren't always sociable. He might prefer to live on his own. You will have to introduce them very slowly and carefully.'

For most cat introductions this would have been good advice. Cats aren't very sociable and just adding another one to a household can lead to quite severe fights. Existing residents usually see a new cat as an intruder on their turf. After all, even among humans, we would dislike it if, after the death of a partner, some strange person moved in as a replacement. People are individuals and a new person cannot be a replacement for a loved one. Cats, likewise, often refuse to treat a new arrival as a friend. So Helen's idea of replacing Lewis with a new kitten wasn't necessarily going to work out well. I told her about swapping scents, introducing the new kitten carefully and slowly, letting Morse smell the new kitten before any contact, and so forth. My advice was good.

It was also wrong! Morse took one look at the new kitten, Frostie, and started grooming him like a mother. That very first day, they curled up together in the cat bed. I felt rather a fool – a feeling quite often induced by cats! The sheer individuality of cats can wrong-foot us so-called experts every time.

Of the three other community nurses I saw, two shared their lives with elderly and much-loved felines, and so they enjoyed meeting my cat during their visits. Tilly, who had originally been absolutely terrified of every human being, became surprisingly positive about the nurses. She would stroll in to see them, usually staying at a respectful distance of about three feet.

She was a carer, too – but only for me. She brought a little daily joy into my life, from the moment when I woke up to her purring to the time when I went to bed with her. She lightened my life but she wasn't much help to Ronnie. She was frightened of his hospital bed, made anxious by his walking frame, and had never bonded as closely with him as with me. She was my cat, not Ronnie's.

Ronnie's growing helplessness was pitiful. About four years earlier he had been diagnosed with prostate cancer and was in remission. Now he had been diagnosed with lung cancer as well, not perhaps a surprise since he had spent most of his life smoking a pipe. As both cancers weakened him, he became very unsteady on his feet. I could no longer rely on friends to help him up if he fell. I had to call an ambulance every time.

Almost every call out involved a trip to the Accident and Emergency Clinic because he usually hurt himself in the fall. I would follow in my car. I began to get used to it. I would ring 999, and while waiting for the ambulance, try to keep him comfortable on the floor with cushions and a blanket. Tilly would usually position herself nearby, looking mystified at why he was lying on the carpet. Then I would pack his medication, remembering to bring the list of his illnesses, in case I forgot one of them.

Each crisis meant an adrenaline rush. Adrenaline would power me throughout the visit, but when we got home several hours later, I couldn't switch off. I would lie awake in the small hours, and when I had to get up to help him to the lavatory that night, the adrenaline rush made it difficult to go back to sleep. I would be high on it for the rest of the 24 hours. Usually, there would be a follow-up visit the next day to another hospital department to deal with any wounds.

Regular visits to the lung-cancer department were required, and other visits for various scans. Luckily, the prostate team had lost interest in him, because he was in remission. There were also occasional trips to the pleural unit, notable for the fact that there you got a cup of tea.

The cancer team decided Ronnie would be given a month's radiotherapy. At this stage, he could still walk in and out of the hospital with his walking frame. I would help him put on a coat and hat for the journey, and put his wallet in his back pocket, because he could not do this while balancing on his frame. I'd take it out again when we returned home.

I walked behind him as he tottered to the car. Then came the worrying moment when I had to help him into the car. I would hold the door open while he manoeuvred carefully into position. Then he would let go of the frame and land almost with a bounce on the car seat. At the hospital, I would position the walking frame outside the car door on the pavement, then reach in and pull him up by a special waist belt. The trick was to embrace him as he moved into a standing position. Sometimes he fell back on to the car seat. Each time I feared he might fall on the hard concrete. From his face, I could tell he shared that fear.

The radiotherapy department was like a little outpost with its own weird culture. The machines were all named Varian One, Varian Two and so on, like science-fiction heroines. Waiting rooms varied according to machine. A small noticeboard in each waiting area told us which machine we were waiting for. If patients didn't notice the noticeboard, they would wait to no avail in the wrong room. The same noticeboard also told us how long we would wait. So did a moving message display at the entrance (also easily missed). Often the noticeboard and the display gave differing information. It didn't really matter as neither waiting time bore any relationship to the real waiting time!

An assessment of the real waiting time came when we found the right waiting room and asked the people already waiting there what the real wait would be. I used to bring a long book with me, but Ronnie could no longer really concentrate on reading. If he picked up a book, he would usually find that his concentration waned after about a page. Sometimes he would listlessly turn the pages of *Hello!* magazine. Often he would just sit. Many of the other people did likewise.

The waiting room was a kind of club. Patients and their partners met each other regularly. There was the tall ectomorphic man with the wife who did crosswords while she waited for him; the man who had to spend 15 minutes gargling with morphine in order to swallow anything; the man with a wife and pretty daughter who looked lovingly anxious. He must have been having treatment for the neck or throat area because he had to be fed through a tube and looked very ill. However, he hadn't lost as much weight as Ronnie had lost, which perhaps was a good sign.

We would arrive and nobody would talk to us or to each other. It was all very British and stiff upper lip. Was that because hearing about each other's pain would be depressing? Maybe it was because people would have to reveal how ill they were. The silence may have been protective or just because Brits don't talk about that sort of stuff. Our waiting room contained predominantly male patients. Perhaps the breast-cancer waiting room, full of women, would have been more chatty.

It was not an unsympathetic silence. All of us would look concerned if one of our number nodded off. Radiotherapy is so exhausting that sleeping in the waiting room was acceptable behaviour. It is thirsty work, too. Several people would repeatedly drink water from the water machine. I would bring milk for Ronnie or sometimes a liquid food, if he had not already drunk his portion earlier in the day. Occasionally, I brought sandwiches. I had to try to keep him eating.

The only change in atmosphere happened one day when two men came in for the first time. They traded a couple of remarks then started a sort of competition.

'I've got gold in my body,' said one of them, a man in his 60s. He had white hair, a jolly, pink face and looked just a little bit overweight. Being a little overweight was a sign of relatively good health. Being very overweight in the radiotherapy waiting room meant steroids. Being underweight rather than overweight meant the cancer was progressing.

'Little bits of gold I've got. I'm worth my weight in gold. They injected me with gold so as to see what happens to it.' He gestured to his pelvic area. Could he really have had gold injected into his prostate? Or gold in his bowel? I couldn't ask.

'*I've* been tattooed there,' said the other, a 70 year old.

A mild man, slightly camp in manner, he told us that he lived with his elderly mother and worked for a local millionaire. He had the deferential manner that marks those still in service as butlers or household staff. 'I don't know how long I shall be able to keep working,' he said. He never did explain why he had a tattoo on his prostate! All of us must have wanted to know but we kept to the proper unspoken rules and did not ask.

On days when he was not having radiotherapy, Ronnie could still walk to his office and read his emails. But just as the cancer was weakening him, so, too, was the treatment. Sometimes he would fall asleep during a conversation.

'It's unnatural to fall asleep all the time,' he admitted. 'It's rather nice but it's feeble. I can't do anything much.'

His weakness increased with each radiotherapy treatment. I wondered if he would be able to get through it without collapse. One morning, just after his treatment was completed, he was in such pain with his ulcerated leg that he could not get out of bed. He had whimpered with pain through the night, even while apparently sleeping. That morning he had to do his bodily functions through his incontinence knickers. He cried with the humiliation.

The next night was worse. At about 6am he had sudden diarrhoea. Thanks to wearing the special knickers, he didn't soil the sheets. I had to get up and help him to the lavatory. Then I cleaned him up and cleaned the lavatory. I was getting good at cleaning up. I had even learned how to clean him up and change his incontinence knickers while he was bedridden. It was always more difficult than cleaning up a cat litter tray.

That night I came in at 4am, and he said goodbye. 'I am reconciled to death,' he said.

I asked forgiveness for my bad temper throughout these last months, and I told him I loved him. I reminded him of how I used to be sick with love, literally. He smiled when he remembered the Piccadilly Hotel in Manchester where we met for an illicit night and I had to vomit first because I was so sick with desire.

Suddenly he said, 'I'd like to get up now.' Then he paused and said, 'I forgot. That was another life.'

Without the help of the palliative nurse, Lizzie, I don't think I could have managed. Lizzie, another cat lover with an elderly cat, Tabitha, found us a hospital bed we could have at home and, in this crisis, she brought in a team of helpers who came three times a day. I didn't quite realize it at the time, but this was the team called in when somebody is likely to die at home. A local charity turned up at nighttime to care for him.

'I'm ready to go,' he told one of them.

She took me aside outside the house as she was leaving, at a distance so that he could not hear us.

'Have you got an undertaker?' she asked.

'No, I haven't.'

'Well, I think you should get yourself a phone number so that you're prepared. When people are ready to go, they often go quite fast.'

It seemed that Ronnie was being poisoned by the radiation therapy that was meant to help him.

There was another painful moment in his journey towards death. I had been given a night nurse for a few days. I was woken by her at 5am. Ronnie was very nauseous. He lay in bed dry heaving with sickness. She called the night doctor and a pleasant and competent African doctor with excellent

English came to see him. He gave him an injection for nausea. A vomiting patient cannot keep down drugs so nausea can, potentially, be very serious indeed.

The next morning, after the nurse had gone, I managed to get most of the pills down Ronnie – little by little by little. I had to wait for him to overcome his nausea at each swallow of water. It took two hours. He no longer wanted to eat but I persuaded him to sip a little of a food drink. He was now living entirely on this liquid. It seemed as if he must be days from death. I had to put his pills directly into his mouth then hold the glass of water to his lips. If he did eat a little normal food, I had to spoon feed him like a baby.

I rang round or emailed Ronnie's friends to say that I thought he was dying. Did they want to come to see him? It was an irony that he was possibly going to die from the radiotherapy that was meant to reduce his cancer.

All kinds of friends turned up to spend a few hours with him. He had a lot of friends. I would leave my place by his bedside and turn it over to them. Ronnie would smile a greeting and talk for a little while. Then the closing of his eyes showed it was time for them to go.

Askold Krushelnycky, a Ukrainian journalist living in New York, caught a transatlantic flight specially to see him. Askold is one of those journalist firemen who turn up in battered suits with a tie in their pocket (in case they have to meet notables) at wars, revolutions (in his case the 2004 Orange Revolution in the Ukraine) and trouble spots.

Like many foreign correspondents, Askold is also an author. He published a book on the Ukrainian revolution, *An Orange Revolution: A Personal Journey Through Ukrainian History.*

He is also romantic, funny and very kind. He once used wire cutters to help free a deer that was trapped in barbed wire down our cart track.

Before he arrived, he had emailed: 'I have told Ronnie myself that he is a hero of mine but I know he probably shies away from being called that. But for me he is a combination of someone from an Arthurian legend and a John Buchan character (except smarter and funnier!). A hero who sometimes weeps is a perfect hero!'

Ronnie wept a little when I read this email out to him and I, who rarely cry, felt pricking in my eyes.

When Askold arrived by hired car, I had lunch ready for him. He looked tired after his overnight flight and the drive from Heathrow airport. While he was eating in the kitchen, I spoon fed some lunch to Ronnie, so that he would not feel humiliated by being seen to eat this way.

'Would you like me to sit with him for a little while,' said Askold after lunch. 'You could take a rest.'

I left him with Ronnie for a couple of hours while I got some badly needed sleep. I could see Askold was slightly worried as he sat by the now-sleeping Ronnie but his determination to help me was touching. I shall never forget his gesture. Like Ronnie, I had developed huge gratitude for small kindnesses.

Were these visits too much for Ronnie? I knew they tired him and I feared they might be too much for him. But would it matter if they hastened his death by a day or two? He deserved these last pleasures, even if they were exhausting him.

My fears were unfounded. Askold's visit was the first sign that Ronnie might recover. He and the other friends who visited that week were a turning point.

At the arrival of each old friend, he would light up and struggle out of the lethargy that the morphine induced to crack jokes with them. The visits made him very happy indeed. I wondered if he was going to rally? At first I reckoned his chances of survival were a mere 20:80. Then I changed this to 50:50. Old friends were literally bringing him back to life.

He didn't die.

I should have realized he would survive when there was a sudden flash of his old humour while I was sitting at his bedside with one of his friends.

He appeared to be in a deep sleep. 'Celia, how will you be able to manage without him?' asked the friend.

'Of course I'll manage,' I replied indignantly, offended that he should think me a helpless woman who could not cope without a man.

'Don't be too sure,' came from the bed. Ronnie had opened one eye and was smiling, before drifting back into sleep. He had heard every word.

Over the next few days he pulled himself back from the brink. He began to eat a little – three teaspoonfuls of porridge, seven de-stoned cherries, a sip of prune juice, and half an ice cream with three strawberries. The following morning he had some scrambled egg, some coffee and half a glass of orange juice. I spoon fed each item singly with a little pause afterwards, in much the same way that I had once enticed Mog to start eating again.

His bowels, so important for the welfare of both cats and men, began performing more normally. The worried discussions between Lizzie and me on the topic of prune juice,

Movicol and other bowel aids bore fruit, so to speak. Litter-tray troubles loom large in the life of the devoted cat owner and this similar human trouble had loomed large for me. It was a relief when his bowels began to function normally again.

'I think I'm well enough to get to my chair,' he said a few days later. Surprisingly, the leg ulcer began to get better, too. His pain came back under control with a careful reassessment by Lizzie and the doctor. Steroids for a few days helped him regain an appetite. Other pills dealt with his nausea.

The special dying-at-home team vanished to help somebody else and we were back to the more normal days. Carers came in to wash him and dress him in the mornings as before. Then I took over for the rest of the time. I felt blessed to have more time with him.

At night I was not willing to put him through the indignities of using his incontinence knickers – they were just there for emergencies. I shared the sofa in the adjoining room with Tilly. She refused point blank to sleep on Ronnie's bed, either at night or in the afternoon. On good nights, I would wake up at about 3am and 5am to help him have a pee. On bad nights, I might have to wake up five times.

At about 6.50 in the morning I would give him his morphine pill, ready for the carers. They came in at 7am and gave him a body wash and dressed him. If he had already had some morphine, these necessary activities were less painful for him. They would help him to the breakfast table on the days when he was able to walk that far.

I cooked breakfast for him and me and made a cup of tea for the carers. Then I would prepare his special drink for bowels, the pill for hiatus hernia, the diuretic pills for blood pressure, the hormone pill for his prostate cancer, the small aspirin as a blood thinner and the other painkillers that he took as well as slow-acting morphine, and a small patch the function of which I did not know.

Finally, after all the pills had been swallowed, I handed him two different inhalers to help his breathing. All this took a long time.

Next, I went upstairs to dress myself. After cleaning my teeth I would bring down the electric toothbrush and help him do his teeth. By now, the diuretics were working and for the rest of the morning I stood by as a lavatory assistant every hour and a half.

When it came to the serious question of bowels, he could now stagger to the lavatory, but I had to help him with his clothes and cleaning up. Then I would clean up the loo if there had been problems – first take off the heightened seat and clean underneath, then clean the tiled floor.

He could not get up or down into his chair without help. Usually, I pulled him up by his belt if he was wearing trousers with a belt. If not, I had to hold him round the chest from the back, remembering not to pull too hard in case I broke his skin. I had a special handling belt, if I remembered to use it, but it was stiff and unhandy to unlock. Later, Lizzie installed a special chair that could tip forward to help him get to his feet.

His whole body was breaking up. The community nurses had to dress the cuts and sores on his arms as well as his leg ulcer. He had huge dark purple bruises on every arm from the steroid injections. His skin was so thin that if I so much as tightened a grip on his arm, it split. Between the nurses' visits, I would dress any new cuts/splits, and re-dress old ones as needed. I became skilful at slowly soaking off the dressings with lukewarm water. If I just pulled them off, his skin came with them.

I put out a liquid food drink at around 10am for him. He rarely wanted the TV on. He preferred Radio Three or Four. Then I helped him through to the kitchen for lunch. Eating was difficult for him. He had congenital tremor in his hands, which meant that he could not eat without bits of food falling off his fork on to his polo shirts. We hit upon the idea of a butcher's striped apron, which he could wear when eating. His shaking hands also meant that he would often spill his food or his cup on the floor.

What was most upsetting wasn't the spill on the floor but the shame and embarrassment he felt at being so clumsy. Seeing him suffer these emotions was heartbreaking. 'My hands are the worst thing about my life,' he said once.

His appetite, such as it was, had reverted to childhood, those pre-war days in Yorkshire with his Primitive Methodist family – sausage and mash, meat pies, Lancashire hot pot and fried fish. His digestion was also breaking up, so I made milk puddings of rice and semolina. These slipped down easily, as did ice cream.

I would then supervise another round of pills before helping him to bed for an after-lunch nap.

I was always tired. Whether this was post-cancer fatigue (it was about a year since my mastectomy), stress (looking after Ronnie) or just lack of sleep (night duties) was not clear. Sometimes I slept after lunch, too, on the sofa, often with Tilly.

I was lucky enough to find a nurse who could come to sit with him for two or three afternoons a week. This was my time off – a whole three hours. At first, I wasted it doing grocery shopping. Then I realized I could do this online from home, and became free to walk.

It had been Tilly's example of self-care that had inspired me the year before to take better care of myself. Walking was the way I did it. I could not go for very long walks in three hours but getting out of the house and walking in the Cotswolds was the way I found a little relief from the stress.

I would arrive home to find Ronnie with a cup of tea and toast, chatting to the afternoon nurse, a friend of mine. She was able to give him some of the encouragement and mental support that I could not longer provide. I was just too tired to be able to look after his emotional wellbeing. I could only look after my own, and I couldn't do that very well.

The regular visits to the local hospital became more and more difficult for Ronnie. From being able to use the walking frame to the car and from the car to the hospital, he became unable to manage the long hospital corridors. Now he could just about walk out of the house to the car, but at the hospital I would get a wheelchair for him. After each visit he would be completely exhausted.

I needed occasional follow-up visits for my own cancer, too. I had been lucky enough to have pre-invasive breast cancer and after a mastectomy did not require radiotherapy or chemotherapy. However, I still needed a check every six months and a mammogram.

Once when our hospital visits coincided, I took Ronnie with me – pushing his wheelchair first down the long corridors to his appointments, then helping him back into the car, out again at another hospital and pushing his wheelchair down more corridors for my appointments. When we got home that afternoon he was so exhausted he could not eat lunch. I was almost as tired as he was and, like him, I was getting more exhausted every day. A nursing home, however excellent, was not the answer. I had to think of something else.

A live-in carer one week a month was the solution, so now a succession of wonderful women would turn up and give me a week's freedom to visit friends or just to get some extra sleep. I still needed to sleep downstairs and look after Ronnie during the night, because they didn't do night duties, but for a week I was no longer housebound.

Luckily, they were all cat lovers! Tilly, who had entirely adjusted to the regular community nurses and indeed to the regular caring team, was slightly less happy about these new people. Nurse visits she could handle, but she was less happy about strangers staying overnight!

So now I had help from the live-in carers for a week each month, the morning carers for the other three weeks, the community nurses, and the nurse who would come and sit with Ronnie in the afternoons – and Gaynor the Trainer, of course.

Most of all I had help from Tilly.

Her presence in the living room was always soothing to me. At first, she had disliked the sofa bed intensely and had insisted on sleeping upstairs on my bed, where I no longer slept. Food was the answer. She was, and is, one of the greediest cats I have ever kept. So all I had to do was sprinkle dry cat food on the sofa bed, before I got into it.

After eating, she would fall asleep on my duvet. And, unlike me, she would usually stay there all night, ignoring me when I got up to help Ronnie. Hearing Tilly's quiet little snore as she slept with me was soothing and, like a lullaby, would sometimes send me to sleep.

She had become the greatest pleasure in my life. My most relaxed moments occurred when I was stroking her little brown and grey tummy, or when I felt her tough, short, black whiskers against my face as she rubbed her cheek against mine.

Now Ronnie needed a cat of his own to cheer him. This cat, I hoped, would be Toby, currently languishing in the cattery until his bowels were sorted out.

Chapter 8

Toby's struggle back to health and happiness

From the beginning it was clear that, despite his cross-eyes, Toby was going to be a handsome cat with his fluffy ginger tail and white whiskers. He didn't have William's wonderful golden eyes circled with a dark circumference, but he had very smart sideburns. He looked like a ginger version of Bradley Wiggins. Well, he would have done but for his dirty ears and the teenage blackheads on his chin. It might be more accurate to say Toby looked like a spotty teenager *imitating* Bradley Wiggins!

I hoped that the arrival of handsome Toby, even if no cat could rival William for sheer beauty, might add interest to Ronnie's life. Ronnie was now so exhausted by the three cancers in his body that he could not leave the house except in a wheelchair. With great effort he could walk from his downstairs bed to his chair in the living room. He got a little weaker every day.

A new cat would be something to watch and perhaps even admire at a distance. Toby was suitable because he had never resorted to scratching or biting when picked up. Even when he was obviously terrified, he had merely frozen stiff rather than fought back. Unlike Tilly, he was a cat who passed the safety test. Tilly, when frightened, could and would administer quite a sharp little bite.

This was important because Ronnie's whole body had developed a sensitivity to pain. If I brushed past him, he winced at my touch. If I pushed him, or prodded him, or stepped on his toe, he literally howled or yelled with pain. The slightest skin contact hurt him and his skin was so thin from the steroids (for prostate cancer) that if anybody had shaken his hand, the skin would have come off like a glove.

Ronnie had chosen Toby's name, just as he had named William. This was promising. Naming an animal is part of claiming the animal, I believe. Why else do people always give new names to rescue cats? A new name is a sign of the start of a new relationship. Better still, Ronnie had insisted, against my wishes, on the name he wanted. If only we could get Toby hygienic and healthy as well as safe.

Thanks to Julie's expertise, he was slowly beginning to recover emotionally and physically. After about a week at her cattery he was using the litter tray without trouble, a necessity if he was going to join a household that included someone with a shattered immune system.

'How did you do it?' I asked her later.

'I put three litter trays in the pen so he couldn't fail to

find one,' she explained. 'I experimented with different kinds of litter. I even tried newspaper instead of litter but it wasn't the litter that was the difficulty for him. I kept all three litter trays very, very clean. As soon as they were used, I would go in and clean them, leaving just a tiny bit of soiled litter so that it smelled right.

'I just persevered. If I caught him coming off the tray, I would reward him with a treat. At first he would pee in one tray and then poo in another. Then he started using just the one tray.'

What is more, it turned out that Toby was warming to Julie. She emailed: *I was in the cattery kitchen washing the cat dishes at the sink when Toby came out of his igloo and went to the tray for a pee. I slowly moved towards his pen and called his name when he had finished. He came towards the door of the pen and looked at me and then looked around before making his way back into his igloo. Not running scared just positive. Good eh?*

Another email later in the same day reported: *I have just done a last walk around the cattery and changed a couple of litter trays and who was sitting in his bed watching me (out of his igloo)? I went to the pen door and talked to him for about five or six minutes and he just looked at me.*

He was also showing signs of friendliness to her brother. Cats are sometimes more frightened of men than women. I had feared Toby might be one of these but I was wrong. He was just frightened of everybody, as many stray cats are. Once, he had lived in a home and been a friendly kitten. He was not a true feral, a cat like a wild animal that had never had human contact. Gaynor and I would never have been able to pick him up if he had been.

He hadn't started life being frightened of people. He had become that way. Thrown out of his original home, he had been shouted at and shooed out of gardens by so many people that he had totally lost his nerve around human beings. His dire experiences living rough had destroyed his trust. His life had hit rock bottom.

While he was at Julie's cattery, I had taken him to the vet for yet another check-up and for his final vaccination. Julie had fished him out of his covered cat bed and put him in the carrier. Getting him out of the cat bed was a problem, even though he was getting to know her. Being skilled with a wide variety of cats, she managed and he did not bite or scratch. He had his second vaccination.

His poo sample had shown that he had a giardia infection – giardia is a nasty little intestinal parasite – so the vet prescribed a paste to be administered three times a day. She also prescribed a special and expensive diet for him. Eating out of dustbins had ruined his digestion, so now he was going to have a lifelong diet that was equivalent in cost to eating out at a five-star hotel.

On the vet's table, Toby froze rather than fighting or running away. He had put on a little weight but when the vet combed him to see if there was flea dirt, huge chunks of hair came out. He was obviously not grooming himself properly. The blackheads on his chin were there perhaps because he was still not castrated. Stud acne, it is called. His ears and the hair growing out of them were dirty, too. He was booked in for the snip on Monday and I planned to bring him home after that.

All the hard work had been done for me by Julie at the cattery. Thanks to her, I could take him home without worrying about his unhygienic habits and the possibility of any chance

138

of infection for Ronnie. I had left one of my own litter trays for him to use in the cattery, so as to get him ready for the move. A familiar tray would help him remember where he should go.

The spare bathroom was now unoccupied during Christmas so that I could keep him there if he had further trouble with the litter tray. Julie's cattery on the other hand was filling up for Christmas, so she couldn't keep Toby any longer. The timing for his arrival at his new and, I hoped, permanent home was perfect. I hoped he would find a quiet bathroom less stressful than a noisy cattery.

The final stage in his rehabilitation was castration. As Ronnie had always found this aspect of cat care troubling, I didn't even tell him about it. Like many men, he didn't like the idea of even an animal losing its sexual equipment. I reckoned it would be better to let him know when the deed had been done. So I took Toby in to the vet direct from the cattery without telling Ronnie about his op, and brought him home in the late afternoon without his ginger bits.

When I carried Toby into the house, I paused in the living room so that Ronnie could see poor sore Toby in the carrier. At this point, aside from looking at the photo on Gaynor's mobile phone, Ronnie had seen Toby, briefly, just once before. 'Yes, he's good looking – handsome, even,' was his approving comment.

I put Toby into the guest bathroom. I had added an armchair to the décor, and covered it with the bed pads I sometimes used for Ronnie. It seemed a good idea to protect the chair in case Toby decided it was a latrine, not a sitting place. For all I knew, he might never have seen an armchair before. Putting him in the bathroom meant that if he missed the litter trays, cleaning up the poo from the vinyl would be easier than cleaning it from carpet. I could also keep a pair of rubber gloves in the bathroom.

The covered cat bed that Toby had been using in the cattery was in the room, too, a hiding place for him that carried his familiar scent. As soon as I opened the carrier he scuttled into this and huddled right at the back of it. I put down a bowl of his expensive prescription food and shut the door leaving him alone to recover from the stress of the journey. Like all new cats he needed a time of quietness to recover from stress.

Early that evening he must have come out to eat his food as a couple of hours later the bowl was licked clean. So I put down another bowl of food. This was also licked clean. Last thing at night I added a handful of dry food, the prescription kind, for a midnight snack. I put some in the cat carrier, as well as in the bowl, so he would start feeling positive about the carrier. He ate all of it overnight, including the biscuits in the cat carrier. Obviously, the operation had not affected his appetite. And then – joy of joys – he used one of the litter trays to pee.

A day later, he used the same tray for poo, as well as pee. That was a relief. It meant he might not need to have two trays all of his own, but I left the extra one there just in case. Twenty-four hours later, after more litter-tray use, I moved him into the spare bedroom. It was December and the nights were getting colder. I reckoned he needed the comfort of carpet, now that he no longer saw it as a potential litter tray.

There was no need to use bed pads any more, since he clearly also knew the difference between litter tray and furniture. In the spare bedroom he would have a choice of beds to sit on, as well as his covered cat bed. I didn't want to introduce him to Tilly, or introduce Tilly to him, until he was fully recovered from his op. Not only did he need to feel well again, but the smell of the vet's surgery needed to wear off. If Tilly smelled the vet on him, she might well take against him from the start. Most cats hate the smell of vets.

While Toby had been at the cattery, Tilly had been having a wonderful time at home. I was slow to understand what was going on. It started when she spent all night walking round the house rather than sleeping on the bed with me. I felt hurt by her rejection of our time together. To wake me in the morning, she made a flying leap on to my chest in sheer exuberance.

Then I realized that she had discovered mice in the house. The first mouse she caught was living behind the Welsh dresser in the living room, not far from the sofa where I now slept in order to care for Ronnie during the night. All through the hours of darkness, she sat near the dresser, waiting for the mouse to emerge. At 6.10am, there was the sound of a cat pounce. I woke to see a happy cat face looking down at me, a mouse's tail hanging down from one side of her mouth. For the next ten minutes, while I cowered under the duvet in case she dropped it on me, she chased that mouse backwards and forwards in the living room. Finally, it disappeared behind the dresser again.

I did not share her pleasure. I was already being woken several times to help Ronnie pee. Now I would be disturbed even more by a mouse-hunting cat. Predictably, all through the next night she sat by the dresser, waiting for the mouse to come out. I slept uneasily, fearing she might jump on the bed to show me the mouse again. By daytime both of us were exhausted. She had a good sleep most of the day. Unlike her, I had things to do.

The third night was even worse. Tilly spent every hour of the night in the utility room, not the living room. I was woken by a crash. She had run into the living room and was racing up and down. I cautiously peered around in the gloom and saw the incriminating tail sticking out of her mouth. She had caught a different mouse, or perhaps the dresser mouse had unwisely moved into the utility room, believing it to be safer.

I shooed her out of the living room, shutting all the connecting doors, and tried unsuccessfully to get her to leave by the front or back door. I guess the cold air outside put her off. It certainly froze me as I stood there with the door open. Instead, she ran up the stairs every time she saw me coming. Planning to release the mouse in my office perhaps? Or the upstairs bedroom?

Finally, in the early hours, after helping Ronnie and listening to various thumps from upstairs, I went into the kitchen to make a soothing cup of tea. When I came back into the hallway, I grabbed a Wellington boot from the utility room and was just in time to catch the mouse, huddled against the wall. Outside in the cold, I shook the mouse out of the boot into the hedge. Maybe a house mouse would survive in the wild, and maybe it would not. At this hour of the night, I did not care.

The next night was calmer. Tilly sat in the utility room, ready to ambush a rodent, but without success. The following night, her persistence paid off. At about 5am I was woken by her running backwards and forwards and under the sofa that was now my bed. Eyes blurred with sleep, I could not be sure what was going on, except I could hear a familiar squeaking. I put on the light and there was Tilly with yet another mouse, a pretty little country mouse with big ears this time, in her mouth.

As I switched on the light, before she could let it go for another romp, I managed to shoo her, mouse in mouth, out of the front door. She ran round and came smartly back inside through the cat flap in the kitchen, which I had forgotten to close. After several unsuccessful attempts to catch it in a Wellington boot again, I shooed her and mouse out of the back door, closed the cat flap both ways, and waited. In the light of the outside bulb, I saw her lose the mouse in a heap of leaves. I dashed out, picked her up and brought her inside.

I was freezing and by now it was four in the morning. I lay shivering with cold for a long time before warming up and going to sleep. As I lay there, I cursed the day that I had taken her into the family. I surmised that she had brought in a pregnant mouse earlier in the year and, well fed on kitchen crumbs, it had produced a litter of little ones. The house had become a sort of game park for cats, where they could hunt at their leisure.

The final episode in the mouse saga took place at midday. I noticed Tilly spending time patting and pulling at the front-door mat. Finally, reluctantly, I pulled up the mat. Below was a thin, squashed and fortunately dead mouse. Here was one she had caught earlier. I must have stood on it as I went out of the front door to pick up the newspapers first thing in the morning. I felt sick at the thought. I picked it up and threw it out.

Tilly was extremely put out. She mooched upstairs and fell asleep on my printer. I envied her these daytime naps. Getting up three times a night meant that I was always short of slumber. Even when I did go back to sleep immediately after caring for

Ronnie, I usually missed out on deep sleep. He would often call for me after just a couple of hours. Being woken up not only by Ronnie but also by Tilly's noisy hunting meant I did not get even the small amount of proper rest that I managed normally. And yet there was something good about it, too. While I was thinking about Tilly, angry about her hunting, or worrying about Toby's reliability in litter trays, I was distracted from my anxieties about Ronnie. For a little time, my mind let go of the minute by minute anxiety about his health.

My greatest fear, which was irrationally growing on me, was how long I could last as a carer. Would it break me emotionally or physically? Would I get cancer for the second time? Ronnie hated hospitals and I did not want him to have to go through a hospital stay again; nor did I want him to end his life in a busy hospital geriatric ward. I wanted him to die at home, with me at his side.

With this in mind, I was cautious about contacting doctors. One night, I had measured his oxygen levels, found them rather low and taken no action. It had been late in the evening and I knew that nobody would be available except the ambulance service. Rather than call them, I had decided to do nothing.

Lack of oxygen wasn't a question of choking or gasping for him. It was just sleepiness. I thought it might be better to let him drift away. If he drifted away during the night, I decided, it might be a good way to go. This would have been a death I wanted for him and a death that he would have wanted for himself.

Was it morally wrong of me to give myself the power of life and death over him, rather than hand this to the professionals? I loved him with all my heart. They didn't. That question haunted me during the night, but it remained unanswered. Luckily (or was this unluckily?) his oxygen levels rose and he woke up in the morning.

All this time, through Ronnie's oxygen crisis and Tilly's midnight hunting, Toby was in the spare room. He slept a lot, as if he was repairing his body and spirit by getting extra rest. He had gone through so much – starvation, two new houses (Gaynor's and mine), a cattery and several veterinary visits. He needed this recovery period. He had healed from his operation, he was using the litter trays reliably and he was clearly less stressed, the proof being that he had taken to sleeping on the bed rather than hiding in his covered cat bed. He had been tested free of FIV or any other infection and he had been fully vaccinated. So far, so good.

It was time to introduce him to Tilly. He was such a small, thin specimen of a cat that he was barely bigger than she was. That was one of the reasons why I had chosen him, or, perhaps I should say, why I had let Gaynor persuade me to choose him. I hoped Tilly would accept him. If she did not, he would find a good home with somebody else, because he was good looking and very gentle. He was much more confident around human beings than Tilly had ever been.

Their first official encounter came when I went upstairs to see Toby in his room and allowed Tilly to come in with me. She was cautious. She padded round the room, sniffed the cat carrier, went inside and ate a few cat biscuits that were there. Then she sat on top of it. Next she inspected the litter tray, which took her nearer to Toby. He slunk tentatively towards her. Neither hissed. The encounter seemed cautious – not hostile but not friendly, either.

I held Toby back from going towards her and he responded to my touch. Tilly retreated from the room. He let me pet him and clearly enjoyed it. Indeed, he rolled on his back and let me tickle his tummy. Many cats dislike having their tummies tickled, so this was confirmation that Toby was rapidly regaining his trust in humans.

It was remarkable how much more relaxed he was at home than in the cattery. Being left alone for several days, apart from visits to feed him and change his litter, had given him the chance to convalesce. He must have found the cattery too noisy, or perhaps he did not like the smell of other cats, and he may have recognized me. After all, he had allowed me to pet him in those first few days when he had been living in my bedroom before being put in the cattery.

This first close encounter gave me a chance to examine him. His tummy fur was thin and showed his pink skin underneath. He had what seemed to be knots or mats near his ears and round his backside. Clearly, he hadn't been keeping his fur in order, and I guess months of not enough to eat, and worms, meant that his coat had become very poor. Poor Toby. He was a real scruff.

He began to play with the catnip mouse that I left in his room, and continued to eat as much of the prescription food as I gave him. He always licked the plate and looked for more. He had not forgotten the times of starvation when he had been happy to eat Gaynor's hedgehog food.

He showed me when it was time to let him into the main house. He began to hang around the bedroom door and try to come out to take a look round. I thought it was time to let him out, too, but Tilly disagreed. She was very cautious and rather worried by him. When he came out and walked into my bedroom, his progress cornered her (not by intent) near the bed. As soon as she could, she ran downstairs.

She came back up later when I rustled the food bowl. She is a cat who will do anything and go anywhere for food. By rattling the food bowl, I was just seeing if she had enough courage to be somewhere in his vicinity, and I discovered that she did. She was cautious and maybe a little fearful, but she wasn't terrified.

Toby was always ready to be petted. He rolled on his back with his legs in the air for a full tummy tickle every time I was near him. His tummy fur was slightly more faded than the dark ginger of the tougher hair along his back. I brushed him gently and huge handfuls of dead fur came out but he still looked like a tramp of a cat and I didn't dare to tackle the mats and knots yet.

His coat felt oddly soapy. If he had been a dog, I would have bathed him. I wondered if this stickiness was something to do with him having been recently fully male. He was obviously not cleaning himself very well. Although he seemed more relaxed, perhaps he hadn't quite settled down and this lack of self-care was a sign of his continuing stress. I remembered that when I first adopted Tilly and she had spent months hiding under the bed, proper careful cleaning occurred only when she felt relaxed enough for it. The other possibility was that Toby's greasiness was something to do with engine oil from when he was sheltering under cars. Perhaps his fur tasted so vile he couldn't bear to lick it.

Even his tail, which looked clean and fluffy, was nothing of the kind. At first, I didn't brush it at all, because it looked so clean. Then, when I ventured to do it, little specks of black came out with the dead hair. Further examination showed that below the apparently clean fluffiness was a hidden layer of grime. Toby had been really filthy.

When I opened the bedroom door to let him out for a little excursion, he would stroll out, stretch his back legs and sort of lope along at a slow pace. His gait seemed rather odd. He was keen to investigate but could be held back. I could still pick him up without any difficulty at all. He never struggled, clawed or bit. Indeed, if I put my hand on his side, he would immediately flop over into what experts call the social roll. Once he must have been an innocent kitten, handled by a family, played with and loved.

The vet had told me that Toby was probably just under two years old. What could have happened in such a short time to turn a happy little kitten into a wreck of a cat, starving to death, with a digestion that could barely cope with food and a coat covered with some kind of greasy muck? Had Gaynor not noticed him eating her hedgehog food, he would have died young.

'I always thought *I* would die young, because of the war and because my mother died when I was only 14,' Ronnie remarked when we were discussing Toby's short and until now unhappy life. 'I'm amazed I'm still alive. It surprises me that I'm so old.'

When I asked him how he coped with being so ill, in so much pain (despite being on morphine) and so disabled, I expected him to tell me what agony he was in. His response surprised me. 'Pain becomes a normal attribute of life and you have to accept it. You sleep a lot because sleep is a relief from pain and this is a pleasurable activity. You become grateful for simple things like warmth and the tolerance of other people. You appreciate people's kindness to you and their forbearance of you.'

There had been a change in him as the cancer took a firmer hold. Once he had been rather intolerant of some people, quick to see them as boring, and quick to avoid people whom he didn't much like. He had always been polite and kind, but now he seemed to have a new, more forgiving attitude to people in general. 'I appreciate small things, like smiles in hospitals and in the supermarket. Complete strangers see that I'm suffering and are nice to me,' he explained.

Some of these small kindnesses stayed in his mind for months. Earlier that year I had taken him to hospital for one of his follow-up visits. He was just about able to get in and out of the car and use his walking frame to hobble into the hospital. It took a long time but he was determined to walk in rather than use one of the hospital wheelchairs.

It was a measure of how weak he was that he was proud of the way he could still manage this. From being a war reporter, struggling to get as near to the frontline as possible, he had become a patient, struggling to walk down a hospital corridor. During one visit, a dirty, gap-toothed woman in her 40s was preceding him into the hospital foyer. When she noticed him behind her, she held back at the doors to make sure they stayed open for him.

'She looked in a pretty bad way,' Ronnie said. 'I think she was drunk, too. But she called me "Darling" as she held back the doors. That meant a lot to me. And then there was the pleural clinic doctor who took over the wheelchair from you and pushed me in himself. These are the kindnesses I notice now.' Far from complaining about, or dwelling on, his plight, he was seeking out the few small moments of brightness.

I wondered whether Toby experienced similar feelings of gratitude. In desperation, he had eaten the hedgehog food, which a well-fed cat might have spurned. He had kneaded with his paws, even when terrified on the vet's table. He had never bitten me, although my combing out of his greasy fur may have hurt him. He had never scratched even when being picked up out of his cat bed in the cattery, which clearly frightened him a lot. Perhaps he, like Ronnie, had learned to endure pain and (in his case) starvation and to appreciate (if not entirely enjoy because of his fear) the kindness of strangers.

Little by little, I let Toby out of his room more frequently and it became clear that while he spent a short time investigating the upstairs rooms, his main preoccupation was to stay within sight of me. Cats don't usually do gratitude but it seemed this cat was the exception. Wherever I went, he would follow me.

I made sure that Tilly and I had quality time together at night. I would feed Toby at 10pm in his bedroom and shut him away for the rest of the night. Tilly would therefore have eight hours in every 24 without his company and she could sleep on my bed undisturbed. I think this helped her to adapt to the situation. I was time-sharing myself.

Toby had not lived in a human home for months, perhaps for almost a year, or more, so he saw nothing wrong with this arrangement. He would bound joyfully into his bedroom for his last meal of the day. Being shut away for the night in a warm room with a bed compared favourably with his nights spent on the concrete under Gaynor's car.

But was he going to be acceptable to Tilly? I wasn't sure and in those first few weeks I told myself that once he was fully recovered, I might rehome him. Maybe I owed it to Tilly that we two should remain closely together undisturbed by a second cat. Tilly had rescued me when I had cancer, taught me that I needed to care for myself if I was going to be able to care for Ronnie.

Whether with me or in a new home there was a bright future for my cross-eyed cat Toby. For Ronnie there was no bright future.

Chapter 9

An upstairs and a downstairs cat

By the time Christmas came, Toby, sheltered from the colder weather and with proper food, was growing healthier. Ronnie, though weakening daily, was almost stable. During other Christmases, I had fostered cats but, luckily, I had no foster cats this Christmas.

It was my physical, rather than my emotional, health that made the festive season of 2011 such a bad one. I had fallen ill first with nausea, then with a throbbing headache, then with a cough. By Christmas Eve, I was feeling sick and unable to eat anything much except porridge. I was losing weight fast and, having survived breast cancer about 15 months earlier, that terrified me. Weight loss is often a sign of undiagnosed cancer. We cancer survivors feel panicked rather than pleased if our weight drops dramatically!

Worse still, I had cancelled the normal daily carers who

came in the mornings to get Ronnie up. Christmas visits had to be booked in advance, so this was a decision I had made about six weeks earlier, when I was still feeling well. I thought it would be nice to have a cosy festive time, just Ronnie and me, without anybody else coming into the house. So the kind and gentle carers did not come on Christmas Eve, Christmas Day or Boxing Day. It was a mistake.

For Ronnie, Christmas was equally dire, although he did not fall prey to whatever virus had attacked me. I felt so bad that I had to wash him in stages on Christmas morning. The first stage was his top half – helping him to sit on the side of the bed with a towel. I then felt so bad that I thought I was going to faint. So I helped him back into bed for another 20 minutes, while I lay on the sofa to recover from the exertion. After that, I washed his lower half. Twenty minutes later I was able to help him into the kitchen where he and I ate some porridge. I just about kept it down.

The day proceeded in a series of rests between caring for Ronnie. Luckily, Christmas had never been a big feast for either of us. Ronnie did not like the annual celebrations of ordinary life – Christmas, birthdays or wedding anniversaries. So, apart from the food, we usually did nothing very much at Christmas.

Between rests, I managed to cook the Christmas goose with one or two dry heaves rather than real vomiting. So I was able to give Ronnie a proper Christmas dinner of goose, roast potatoes and red cabbage. I made the effort because I feared this might be his last Christmas on earth. I couldn't eat anything, but Tilly and Toby benefited from some of it. By now, Ronnie ate only tiny amounts, no matter what food he was given.

The day got even worse when I found a dying mouse

under the vacuum cleaner. Its tail was half bitten off, its lower half was paralysed but the poor thing wasn't dead. Tilly must have brought it in, or she had discovered it living in the house and decided it would be a nice Christmas gift for me. I did not appreciate it. I swept it into a Wellington boot and put it in the hedge to die in peace. It would have been kinder to kill it with a brick but in my current state of nausea I just couldn't face doing that.

Toby was not responsible for the mouse but he was growing in confidence. He no longer needed to hide in his covered cat bed when I came into the bedroom where he was living. In the mornings, he would zoom out with enthusiasm, making tiny kitten noises when I opened the door. He had been waiting, eager for release, no doubt alerted by my footsteps on the stairs. Now I let him out for longer periods.

I had already started swapping his scent with Tilly's scent. In the first stage, I took two cheap, small blankets and put one on the bed where he slept, and one on my sofa bed, where Tilly slept, exchanging them daily. The idea was that both blankets would smell of both cats so that each blanket passed on the scent of the cat who had last used it.

The next stage was to spread their joint scent round the house. I took a clean hanky and gently rubbed it against Tilly's cheek and then Toby's cheek, mixing their scents together. Then I rubbed the hanky, at cat height, on the various parts of the house and furniture where I had seen Tilly rubbing. I was creating what I hoped would be a harmonious family scent of both cats. I did this both downstairs and upstairs as often as I remembered.

On Boxing Day, Toby still hadn't come downstairs despite

all this scent mixing, and I was still ill enough to find any exertion difficult. I had also lost my voice and could only croak when people rang me to see how I was. That day, Tilly gave me a real fright. The first I heard was a cry from Ronnie on the lavatory. 'Help, Celia. Help.'

I thought he might have fallen off the lavatory bowl, or maybe his bowels were not working properly, but when I rushed in, Ronnie was securely seated on the lavatory. Tilly, however, was dodging between his legs in pursuit of yet another mouse. Luckily, it had not run up his legs to escape her. I managed to inveigle it into a Wellington boot and freed it in the garden.

Tilly was not pleased, but I felt no sympathy for her. There seemed no end to her hunting. Bringing in living mice and letting them go was fun for her but simply contributed to the household population of mice. So much for the idea that cats keep a house mouse-free. 'We never had mice in the house until we got cats,' Ronnie reminded me again from the lavatory.

During Toby's investigations in the upstairs rooms on Christmas Day, he had passed Tilly twice and she hadn't felt the need to run away. Later on in the day, however, he blundered up to her and got so close that she had to hiss at him to persuade him to move back to a polite distance. It was like seeing a bad-mannered teenager meeting a sensible grown-up woman.

On the Saturday after Christmas, Toby eventually ventured downstairs to investigate the rest of the house. He did a quick flip round the living room before retreating back upstairs. Now, at last, Ronnie could see him. I can't say that Toby was looking his best. His body hair was still very tatty, although his fluffy tail, with its dirt hidden, looked attractive, as did his sideburns.

'He's personable,' Ronnie surprisingly remarked. Obviously, he had taken a liking to this pathetically thin cat.

On his next excursion to the living room, I picked up Toby for a closer inspection. The knots and mats down his lower flank and inside his thigh were still there. He had not groomed them out. His breath smelled foul. Poor little cat. He was keen to have my attention and would roll over if I put my hand under his tummy. So I managed to cut away a few of the knots that I could reach easily.

He was frightened by the scissors and I could have cut him by mistake if he had wriggled too hard. So I decided I would take him to the vet for a shave under a mild anaesthetic. Despite my asking for this, the nurse at the vet's surgery merely combed out the knots. Within two days ten knots were back again.

The whole procedure had been a waste of time and money. Usually, knots that are combed out don't return that quickly, if at all. I could only assume that something bad tasting and virulently sticky had got on to Toby's fur. If he had cooperated by grooming his combed fur, the knots might not have re-formed. At this stage he did not do grooming.

Perhaps he had been spraying, as entire tomcats do, and his urine had blown back on his body. This might have the effect of a kind of aftershave, attractive to females but sticky on his coat; or perhaps he had fallen into something slimy and, because he didn't groom it off, it had stayed on his coat. I worried that his refusal to groom might be the result of something wrong in his mouth – gum disease perhaps.

When my cat-loving nephew, Jess, visited a few days later, he held Toby while I carefully cut out every single knot with scissors. Toby looked rather ragged, but who cared about that? In Jess's firm grip, Toby stayed compliant, if unhappy, throughout.

'Shall we bathe him?' I asked Jess. I had bought a weird and expensive concoction called Groomer's Goop.

'I don't think so,' Jess replied. 'It seems cruel to put him through the trauma of being washed.'

So we waited for Toby to wash himself.

He was now using his litter tray twice a night and three times a day in small, but not tiny, amounts. Could this be the beginning of cystitis? I looked for signs of blood in the urine but there were none. Peeing smallish amounts turned out to be just a personal eccentricity of his.

He was turning out to be a cat with some odd habits. He never dug into the litter, and he never covered up what he had eliminated. Maybe he had stopped digging when he had to eliminate on concrete or paved carports. From my point of view, his refusal to dig was a bonus – less litter scattered on the carpet.

He started taking regular trips downstairs, retreating into his bedroom when he felt scared. He literally slunk around, his body low to the ground. The kitchen with its food smells was understandably his favoured place but he also spent time with us in the living room.

'I don't think he is used to television,' remarked Ronnie one evening. Toby was clearly anxious about the TV. At first, he just kept away from it but that evening he had dared to approach the screen, peering at a Channel 4 discussion and then retreating to the side of Ronnie's chair, looking worried. Perhaps if it had been a wildlife programme he might have stayed longer. Later on, he became a fan of Chris Packham's programmes!

Ronnie put down his hand for the fearful Toby to touch and exclaimed, 'Toby bit me – just a little nip.' I found that difficult to believe because Toby was very gentle with me, even when I was snipping off his matted fur. There were no tooth marks or bruising on Ronnie's hand. Ronnie's body, painful each time I touched him, had responded badly to just the merest feline touch. Maybe a friendship between Ronnie and Toby wouldn't work out if any direct contact hurt Ronnie.

Rehabilitating Toby was going to be more complicated than I had thought. Toby's temperament was fine, but his bodily condition was still really bad. I worried about almost everything – whether Tilly would be happy with Toby, whether I was betraying her trust by adding him to the household, whether I would have to upset Ronnie by rehoming Toby.

These worries kept me from falling asleep at night, and stopped me getting the sleep that I so desperately needed. But worrying about the cats blocked out my biggest worry – that I would fail Ronnie in his darkest hour. I wanted so desperately to care for him until the end of his life and to protect him from the kind of death my mother had experienced. The cats were a welcome distraction from this.

Fortunately, a few days later, Toby exhibited the first signs of feeling relaxed enough to start grooming. Most cats leave their tail to last, beginning with their face and grooming downwards. Toby started his toilet with his tail, possibly because it was the least sticky part of his fur. The tail had never developed knots; or perhaps he started there out of a kind of pride. His tail and sideburns were the most glamorous parts of his coat.

I had already brushed this tail thoroughly and most of the

specks of car or diesel dirt had now gone. Toby took up the task of clearing the final ones with a careful persistence. He would sit on the sofa, holding down his tail while he groomed it. The tail with its white patches at the end grew cleaner and fluffier by the day. It had always been a fine tail. Now it was a magnificent one.

The next part of his body that he attended to, a day or two later, was his face. I noticed him licking his front paws and wiping them round his chops. His tummy was next. Toby's tummy is coloured like a redhead's skin. It is pink and if he were human, it would be freckled! His tummy fur is soft, much softer than normal short cat fur, but much sparser than the rest of his coat. There are no thick guard hairs. Toby was happy to show off his stomach under all circumstances. At the slightest excuse he would roll over enthusiastically exposing his pink tum.

Some of the worst knots, which I had cut off with scissors, had been on the inside of his thighs in that softest of fur. Toby now began to do proper tummy fur maintenance. Sometimes he lay on his back and just twisted forward to lick his lower chest. At other times he took up that amazing cat position whereby one leg goes over the shoulder and the cat can lick its bottom. By now, he was doing the full grooming sequence, attending to every part of his body. Only his chin with its blackheads and his ears with their waxy hair stayed dirty.

Tilly, when she finally adapted to my home, had spent a lot of time grooming. Toby was doing the same. The Groomer's Goop would not be needed. The sign of a recovering cat is self-care. Tilly had taught me that, after I rescued her. Now Toby was slowly recuperating from his ordeal on the streets and was literally grooming away all signs of it.

In contrast, Ronnie was slowly deteriorating. His cancers in the prostate, bone and now in the lungs, were either in remission or controlled for pain, but a whole series of small but distressing disorders continued to plague him.

The day after Toby first ventured downstairs, Ronnie had started bleeding while he was on the lavatory. He hadn't passed a motion for 48 hours and was refusing to take his normal laxative drink. I had alternately to bully and coax him into taking a double dose.

The next part of his anatomy to suffer was his eyes. He fell prey to conjunctivitis, an eye infection that went away when treated but usually returned a few weeks later. He got fungal infections, such as athlete's foot, in his groin, a shaming area for any man. It was as if his body could no longer cope, and could not protect itself from these minor ills. I became expert in rubbing on ointment and adding paper hankies to try to keep the groin area dry. There appeared to be no long-term cure, but after a couple of months it healed itself.

Then he developed a hard and painful lump in his inner thigh. That necessitated yet another hospital visit, because I feared it might be some kind of new cancer, but the hospital nurse declared it was just an abscess and drained it. After that, I had to drain it every day until the blood flowed. It took several weeks to go away. Ronnie never complained but I could see that it was yet another humiliation for him. His lover and wife had become his nurse, and he was very unhappy about it. He also suffered emotionally from seeing me so exhausted.

He told a friend, 'She has recovered from breast cancer much more slowly because of all she has to do for me.' He did not talk to me about this because he knew how much I hated it if he cried. One of the ways he looked after me emotionally was to try not to cry in front of me.

For the first week or two that Toby was free to leave his bedroom as he chose, I had an upstairs and a downstairs cat. Toby spent most of his time upstairs and made occasional visits downstairs. Tilly was the downstairs cat, spending much of the day and all the night with me on the sofa. As Toby grew in confidence, he came downstairs in the daytime, too.

I was taking no chances with him. I feared that he might run away if I left the cat flap open, so I locked the cat flap and let Tilly in and out by the kitchen door. Like many cats, she had always preferred to have the door opened rather than having to push the cat flap. It seemed right and proper in her eyes that I should act as a doorman and commissionaire. So a change from a cat flap to doors being manually opened was no hardship to her.

When, finally, I dared to open the door for Toby, it became clear that the precaution of a closed cat flap was entirely unnecessary. Toby had no plan to run away. Indeed, he had no intention of going outside the house at all. He had learned to use the litter tray and had decided that a litter tray was infinitely preferable to a cold flowerbed. He had no interest in the garden. Clearly, he wanted to stay in a warm house.

Fresh air had no appeal for him whatsoever. I couldn't get him to go outside on his own. He would hover anxiously at the door, if I opened it, refusing to put a paw over the threshold and looking back at me to make sure I didn't shut him out. If I walked up the garden, he would follow me for a few yards, then halfway up he would give a series of pitiful mews and refuse to go any farther. When I turned to go back, he would shoot back into the house. He really didn't want to do the great outdoors at all. Living in the open under cars had nearly killed him. Not only had he been cold and wet, he had also been near starvation. Indoors, with two meals a day, was where he wanted to remain at all costs.

Some stray cats feel safer outdoors than inside, at least to begin with. My first cat, Fat Ada, had been one of them. When stressed, she would make a bolt for the door. Toby was clearly going to be the opposite. As he stood hovering in the doorway, I could almost see the bubble coming out of his mouth, which read: 'I've done outdoors and I didn't like it!'

During January the weather grew colder. I was still feeling ill. This was a long-lasting virus. It started snowing and the live-in carer arrived a day early for her week. As the snow mounted, I could no longer drive down the cart track. The snow lay four feet deep and drifted off the fields, banking up the hedge down the track. We were properly snowed in.

I started feeding the birds in my garden with bread, as well as birdseed. The idea of extra free food excited Toby's curiosity and he deigned to set a paw outside the house for the first time without my company. In pursuit of the bread, he would go as far as the bird table, gobbling down the larger crumbs.

For a cat with impaired digestion, living on carefully formulated prescription foods, this should have been disastrous, but far from it. Toby's digestion might not have been able to cope with ordinary cat food, but dry bread suited him fine. He had obviously adapted to a diet of scraps while living on the street. His digestion could cope with junk food. With the exception of his expensive prescription diet, it was the good food that upset his stomach.

Tilly had met snow before and enjoyed chasing leaves. She would range quite far, sometimes walking up the track to spend a couple of hours hunting in the nearby barn. She was happy to sit under cover near the garden shed and look out at what was happening around her. She was semi-longhaired and so could tolerate a little snow on her coat without getting too cold.

Toby's hair, though coarser, was also semi-long but he had no desire to play in the snow, even though he had a natural fur coat to keep out the cold. He only went out to steal the birds' food. He would pick his way carefully, placing each paw on any patches of grass that were relatively free from snow. Even icy patches were preferable to soft snow.

Occasionally, he would pause to shake the snow from each paw or to shake off any flakes that had landed on his back. Bird footprints were carefully inspected. Any crumbs were eaten up. He never went far and his trips outside lasted for just a few minutes. Then he would beetle back inside again to the warm kitchen as fast as possible.

I did not go very far, either. A year earlier, when we had been snowed in over Christmas, I had walked with pleasure to the local village shop – a round trip of about an hour and a half. This year I did not feel well enough to do so. Instead, I spent my afternoons sleeping upstairs while the carer sat with Ronnie. Tilly shared the bed with me upstairs.

As Toby was feeling well and full of beans, I opened the cat flap, using a clothes peg so he could come and go without having to push. Even so, Toby seemed unable to understand how even an open cat flap worked. This might explain why he had fared so badly as a stray, I thought. More cunning stray cats use cat flaps to break into houses and eat the food left down for resident cats. What I hadn't really understood was that even if Toby did know how to use a cat flap, he was not going to leave a warm house, although the kitchen was cold while the cat flap was permanently open.

Ronnie, who like most people was not good at interpreting cat behaviour, said he had seen Toby 'playing' with Tilly. 'He was chasing her in fun,' he said. This did not seem likely to me. He was more likely to be bullying her.

The following morning, after I had let Toby out of his bedroom and fed both of them separately, she came upstairs with me when I was cleaning my teeth and Toby followed us. He crouched and looked as if he was going to pounce on her – predatory behaviour that worried me a lot. I intervened and shut him out.

'I'm not sure I can keep him if this behaviour continues,' I told Ronnie.

'You can't get rid of him. He's part of the family,' Ronnie replied. 'When he goes out more, some of his surplus energy will be used up outside, slaughtering wildlife,' he added optimistically.

Toby's attitude to Ronnie was benign but not very interested. Ronnie, after all, could not feed him. As I was the feeder, he concentrated most of his winning ways upon me. He would roll at my feet in doorways so I had to stop to tickle him. He would pursue me into the lavatory. He would make a series of tiny abandoned-kitten noises if I went out of his sight. He followed me downstairs to the kitchen in the morning, upstairs while I did my toilet, then downstairs when I sat with Ronnie.

In his eyes, I was his saviour. Toby's reaction to me was the only time I have seen feline gratitude in full action. Most of my cats have taken my affection for granted. Their attitude has been that they were owed my attention. In their eyes, our relationship had been one of human deferring to cat.

Emotional dependence doesn't suit cats. I feel they should be independent by nature. I hoped that Toby's addiction to me would be a passing phase. In a way, I hoped it wasn't gratitude. I hoped he was just keeping close to his food source. Could it be that he feared he might be abandoned again? By keeping me in sight, was he making sure that I didn't desert him like his earlier owners? Being trailed round the house by a whimpering cat was flattering but not what I really wanted. Besides, Toby was meant to be Ronnie's cat.

The major problem in their relationship was his doglike devotion towards me. He trailed round behind me and would literally push Tilly away, interposing his body between her and me. He was intensely possessive. I had hoped he would concentrate his affection on Ronnie, not me. If I had wanted a co-dependent pet, I would have got a rescue dog not a cat.

After the carer's week, when Ronnie and I were alone again for the next three, I started encouraging Toby to get on to Ronnie's bed during the afternoon. Tilly had never shown any inclination to do this and if I lifted her up on to the bed, she would promptly jump off. Besides, Tilly sometimes scratched. If she was anxious, or if by mistake she was hurt, she would retaliate with her claws. She was not a safe close companion for a man whose skin bled at the slightest touch.

Toby, on the other hand, never bit or scratched, even when it was clear he was terrified. Despite Ronnie's earlier claim that Toby had nipped him, I felt he would be safe in Toby's paws. And now that Toby was reliably litter trained, clear of fleas and generally healthy, there were no hygiene issues. It was time to see if he and Ronnie could bond a little.

First, I tried lifting him on to Ronnie's lap as Ronnie sat in his chair. That didn't work at all. Toby simply jumped off. Like most of my cats, he didn't do laps. Indeed, Toby wouldn't even sit on *my* lap. I could bribe him on to my knee with a treat. He would eat it and leave. I could hold him on my knee and he would sit there submissively while his whole body tensed, ready to leap off at the first opportunity.

It wasn't that he hated being near me. He would cuddle up close to me on the sofa, either while I watched TV in the evening or while I slept in the afternoon. His idea of bonding was to sleep with his body touching mine, just like friendly cats do with each other. Perhaps sitting on my lap seemed unnatural to him, while sleeping side by side was the proper cat thing to do.

So it seemed to me that the best way to help him and Ronnie become friends was to use the afternoon when Ronnie was sleeping as bonding time. I would be nearby, resting on the sofa, to intervene if anything went wrong. It didn't. The first time I lifted him on to Ronnie's high hospital bed, Toby snuggled down immediately on top of the duvet, aligning himself alongside Ronnie's body.

He showed sensitivity to Ronnie's pain and would simply arrange himself where there was space, instead of inching his way into the centre of the bed as many cats do. Since he was on top of, not inside, the duvet, he never actually touched Ronnie's body, which by now seemed to hurt at almost any touch. The duvet was a safe barrier.

He also remained very still, far stiller on Ronnie's bed than on the sofa with me. As the two of them drifted off to sleep in the afternoons, I could see from Ronnie's expression that Toby was a comfort to him. I could leave them there together safely, even when I wasn't in the next room.

If Ronnie woke and called for me, I would lift Toby off. Then when Ronnie was back in bed, I would put Toby back on the bed and he would just settle down again. He was not a cat who wanted to be out and about, doing things. At this stage in his life he was only too happy to do nothing at all except sleep.

Sometimes I would look in and see him stretched out on his back, his ridiculous fluffy pink tummy lined up parallel to the shape of Ronnie's body under the duvet. He adjusted happily to this routine, waiting to be picked up. He could not jump up of his own accord, because the bed was very high and because he seemed to have weak back legs.

He would accompany Ronnie in the living room during the day when I was busy about the house or upstairs at my computer. There wasn't room for him on Ronnie's chair and he did not want to be on his lap, so he would sleep on the nearby sofa or on one of the other two armchairs. Toby provided much-needed company for Ronnie, and I was to discover almost a year later that Ronnie enjoyed photographing him with his iPad.

'Toby is a carer in a way. He cheers me, he really does,' said Ronnie. 'I like his little tricks, his antics, and it's nice to have something pretty to look at.'

By now, Ronnie felt so ill that he refused to see any more visitors who sought his company, except one or two who lived locally. 'I don't want them to see me like this. I want them to remember me as I was,' he explained. 'I'll just close my eyes and refuse to speak if you inflict them on me.' He felt a kind of shame at being so ill, so disabled and clearly so unable to cope.

The visitors, anyway, had now decreased in numbers. Those who had come to say goodbye earlier, naturally felt little need to repeat the process. Some people could not face visiting at all, unable to bear seeing Ronnie laid so low. Visiting the dying involves facing up to human mortality. Many people cannot do this. Once the whole world had been his journalistic playground. Now it had shrunk to two rooms.

So Toby's silent companionship was important. Just as Candy the nursing-home cat had pleased my mother in her last days, so Toby was providing the same comfort for Ronnie. His presence required no effort on Ronnie's part. He took my place as Ronnie's afternoon sleeping partner, just as Tilly had taken Ronnie's place with me on the sofa at night.

The days and weeks and years when Ronnie and I had slept in the same bed, often in each other's arms, were gone forever. Now I slept with Tilly and in the afternoon he slept with Toby.

Chapter 10

Therapy cats

At night, Toby was still sleeping in the spare bedroom with the door firmly shut. I was anxious that Tilly should have her time with me alone. The relationship between them was beginning to worry me. One reason for this was their relative size. I had chosen Toby because he was small, almost as small as Tilly.

Now he was growing. At first, despite eating everything I gave him, he had not put on any weight at all. Indeed, he had lost weight under my care. A diagnosis of malabsorption and expensive prescription food had changed this. The vet's scales showed his weight had reached 4kg and she considered he should be about 4.3kg, so I allowed him to eat as much as he liked. By now, he had cost about £800! I could have got a pedigree kitten for that sum – not that I would have done so.

No longer gaunt and thin, Toby's health was improving along with his looks. I was feeding him three times a day, instead of the twice daily food that Tilly received. The first sign of his recovery was his fur. It was now clean and fluffy and thicker. Only on his tummy was the soft, fluffy fur a little sparse so that his pink skin could be seen through it. His haunches, however, were still painfully sticking out, but his breath no longer smelled so vile. Considering how much he ate, twice the amount allowed Tilly, his weight increased very slowly. It was as if his body needed the food to repair him internally first.

Then he started to grow – and he grew and grew. I might have realized this would happen by looking at his paws, which had always been large compared with his skinny body. He was now growing as, under other circumstances, he would have done as a younger cat. He was, so to speak, growing into his paws. The vet had said he was about two years old, but when he suddenly put on weight, it began to look as if he might have been younger than that. He was having a delayed adolescent growth spurt.

Also, after castration, his body shape began to change. Instead of the heavy front quarters and slender back quarters of a masculine tomcat, he had put on weight at the back. He was still a little odd in his back quarters, as if he might have been hit by a car in the past. I decided not to take him to the vet for an X-ray – it would be better for him to have several months of quiet living without visits to the vet.

He was never going to become a large cat, like a Maine coon, or even one of those big heavy British Blue tomcats, but he was now a medium-sized cat, and thus much larger than poor little Tilly, who remained tiny, with tiny paws and a tiny body. Tilly was fully grown, with lustrous brown-grey fur and a neat little black face. She would never become larger, although judging by the signs of tummy sag, she might become fatter! The only legacy of her neglected and starving kittenhood was a slightly weepy left eye, possibly the result of cat 'flu in early life.

Apart from the slightly odd gait in his back legs, Toby had two remaining problems, acne and dirty ears. His chin was dark with blackheads. I tried to deal with them by buying cleansing acne pads for humans (as my vet had recommended for William a few years back). I put Toby on my lap and started to wipe his chin.

He did not enjoy it, wriggling hard, but where I had cleaned, fewer blackheads remained. I hoped they would not re-emerge. He still had testosterone in his system, which was clearing slowly after his castration, and some people believe stud acne occurs as a result of male hormones, just as adolescent humans suddenly sprout spots at puberty. If that was so, as his male hormones died away altogether, he might become free of acne. I hoped so. Then I remembered that William, castrated as a kitten, always had a few spots of acne on his chin.

I changed from using human skin wipes to using an antiseptic lotion used by vets. This was slightly less unpleasant for Toby. I would wipe it on, use the flea comb, then wipe it off with a dry pad. The flea comb and the pad would both be full of black spots but some always remained. A full set of spots usually re-emerged after a mere four days. Toby was just naturally spotty.

The charming tufts of hair that grew out of his ears had grown by about half an inch but they were still dirty with earwax. The vet had cleaned inside the ears using a cotton bud, but I was reluctant to risk this. I might do him harm by mistake. If only he had been able to reach his chin or his ear hair, no doubt he would have cleaned up both the acne and the earwax, but he could not clean his ears, even if he wanted to. Earwax and blackheads might look bad, but they were not a sign of ill health, so I decided I would not harass him about his ears, and only tackle his acne when it grew too thick and horrible.

One area of his body was a complete revelation – his white whiskers. They grew and grew. They had always been longer than Tilly's short black whiskers. Now they were huge and glorious like his fluffy tail. From being about four inches, they were now almost seven inches long. They drooped like a Turkish bimbashi's military moustache – thick, strong and slightly curved.

With these huge whiskers, magnificent tail and clean fur, it became clear that Toby was ginger and gleaming white rather than ginger and dirty white. So I had a handsome ginger and white cat with permanently dirty chin and ears. Like some spotty adolescent youth, he was a mixture of glamour and squalor!

'I shall call him Kevin,' I said to Ronnie.

'Don't you dare,' he objected. 'Toby is his name. He's not a Kevin.'

So Toby he remained. By now, Ronnie had been entirely won over by Toby's gentle snoring in the afternoon on his bed. Toby was now definitely Ronnie's cat.

To see Toby looking so well and vigorous was wonderful, but it was also slightly disquieting. I had taken him in partly because he was so small and weak that I believed he would not be able to bully Tilly. Now that he was larger, much larger, the disparity in their size gave him a huge advantage over her.

When he first started sharing the house with her, he had sometimes been bullied by her. When he was pushy – shoving his nose too close to hers, or up her bottom, which she disliked – she would turn round and face him off. He would sit in the hall, producing a series of sad little miaows, while she was in the living room with me. I was not sure if he was frightened of her, or of the TV.

Then their relationship started changing. I had never expected them to become close friends. Cats usually only do friendship if they have been introduced to each other as kittens. Occasionally, two adult cats will bond, and occasionally, an adult cat will take to an introduced kitten, like Morse adopted Frostie. But most of the time, they do not become buddies. They just learn to live in the same house, feline courteous avoidance substituting for real liking.

This is what I was hoping for. I had introduced them carefully and slowly so there had never been a fight. As the resident cat in her own territory, Tilly had been intrigued, anxious but never hostile to Toby, except when he got too close to her. At times she would stand up to him, at other times she would run.

One fairly typical encounter occurred later, when I was sitting at the top of the stairs, feeding Toby cat biscuits while I tried to brush him. I brushed both him and Tilly almost every day. Tilly must have been attracted by the sound of food and sneaked into the bedroom behind my back. Toby heard her and followed her into the bedroom. Then Tilly came running out and down the stairs. On this occasion, I managed to intercept Toby's pursuit of her.

This was not what I wanted. I hoped Tilly would at least sometimes stand her ground, but as he grew, she decided that she would not risk doing this. He was now bigger, much bigger, than she was. Her feline common sense ruled out standing up to a cat twice her size. When he was shut away at night, she took on a look of bliss and would immediately collapse on her back with her legs apart in front of me. The bubble coming out of her head would say: 'Thank goodness that ginger moron is not here and we can be together at last.'

During the day, a cycle of chase behaviour had now started up. The more Toby chased, the more Tilly ran. And the more Tilly ran, the more Toby chased. She would run at the slightest possibility that he might interfere with her and, as soon as she turned tail, he pursued her. I could tell from his demeanour that he enjoyed chasing her. He never caught her and he never, ever, hurt her.

For him, chasing was always good fun. He chased leaves. He would chase up and down the garden when I was with him, half running up trees. Sometimes he would just run up and down the garden in an aimless way.

But was being chased fun for her? The central problem was access to me. Jane, the lovely New Zealand carer who came to live in for a week to help me with Ronnie, fell in love with Toby. She particularly liked the way he would lie with his tongue hanging out when he was happy. She reported his every move when I was not in the house. 'He doesn't chase Tilly when you're out,' she said.

I could hardly believe it. Then it made sense. It wasn't that Toby had too little to do. His determination to keep Tilly away from me accounted for much of the chasing.

I was also reassured by my friend, novelist Celia Brayfield, when I visited her during Jane's week with us. Celia and I share not just a first name but a love of cats. In the days when we all submitted paper manuscripts to publishers, hers, like mine, always had a few cat hairs and several paw prints on them. She has a robust attitude to her two cats, handsome black Scaramouche and Siamese cross Timoute aka Tim.

Her cats are more or less upstairs and downstairs cats. At the time of my visit, Scaramouche had won the privilege of going upstairs, and was refusing to let Tim go there. It did not worry her. 'I think it's good for their characters to have two cats in a household. If you have just one solitary cat, it will rule your life,' she said. Of course, this ignores the fact that two cats can rule one's life just as easily but we cat lovers are often in denial about being controlled by our cats. So her remarks were comforting.

Toby and Tilly seemed like a friendly couple when they were united by a common interest. When I returned from seeing Celia, both of them thought there was a mouse under the cooker. So did I. It seemed only too likely that Tilly might have brought one in. Tilly just sat and looked intently. Toby, despite being larger, actually crawled underneath it – something that Tilly had never done. He managed to wriggle in a space just four inches high, even though by now he was about three times that height at his shoulder. That particular mouse was never caught. Perhaps it died there.

I alternated between hope and anxiety about them. My hopes of a sensible relationship between the two would rise when I saw them sleeping in the same room, admittedly far apart. One evening they even sat either side of me on the sofa. On another occasion, Toby came out with Tilly into the garden with me. He chased her up a tree – nothing special in that. Then *she chased him up the same tree.* I was thrilled.

The very next day, he chased her out of the house in front of my eyes. The sequence was this. Toby was in your face towards her, making her uneasy. He came up towards her, just too close for her comfort. She ran. He ran after her. The situation seemed to be that any quick movement by her set off his chasing.

I decided he needed more chase games and experimented with an old fishing-rod toy that had a fake goldfish on the end. He went mad for it. If I gave him about an hour of playing with this, he was slightly better about Tilly. But even with extra games (and an hour is a long time to be playing with a cat) he still refused to let her come too near me. He guarded me like a dog guards a bone.

On one occasion, when she was lying on her side, he came next to her and rolled on his side to lie down, too. He was so close that his body was touching hers. She got up and left, clearly uncomfortable with his closeness. I think he did it deliberately to make her move away. She came back after a moment or two and looked as if she was going to go for his throat as he lay there. She stood over him, then walked away. His non-aggressive but pushy move had succeeded.

When he wasn't sleeping, Toby spent most of his time trying to get my attention and prevent me giving it to Tilly. Sometimes a mere glance from him would stop her coming towards me. Cats can do intimidation with a single stare. However, it was never absolutely clear how far she was a complete victim. Despite being chased, it seemed that she might be able to cope.

I was reassured to discover that, when it came to food, she lost all fear. I was in the habit of giving Toby an extra lunch – a whole handful of cat biscuits. To do this, I would shut him in his room where he would be undisturbed by her. Shortly after the episode of the mouse under the cooker, when I came to let him out after his lunch, she came out, too. She had sneaked into the room and hidden. Who knows who had eaten the biscuits. Him? Her? Both of them?

When it came to theft, they would tolerate each other and perhaps even cooperate. I came home from a short shopping trip (less than an hour because I had no carer) to find they had managed their first joint enterprise in feline wickedness.

There were 20 small pieces of bread and one half slice on the kitchen floor. Toby did not yet have the confidence to jump up on kitchen surfaces, so Tilly had to be the one who had pulled the slice out of the plastic bag and nudged it onto the floor. Both cats were eating the bread, side by side. Toby's contribution may have been to tear the slice into small pieces to make it easier to eat. Normally, when Tilly stole dry bread, she would just eat from the edge of a slice.

This was yet another humbling moment when I realized how little I knew about cats. I was meant to be a cat behaviour expert and here were my cats misbehaving. Admittedly, I had made no effort whatsoever to keep them off the kitchen surface. While I did not encourage this behaviour, Ronnie had always enjoyed it. He liked an attendant cat on the kitchen table while he ate. And I have to admit that I did, too, and still do.

'Look at this,' he called to me one afternoon at teatime. Toby had leaped on to the arm of Ronnie's chair, reached over and pulled a piece of toast and Marmite out of Ronnie's shaking hand, leaped down again and run into the kitchen to eat it. Ronnie laughed.

Anything that made poor Ronnie laugh was OK by me.

Tilly was already a committed food thief, having been brought up in kittenhood on takeaway food, such as chips, fish batter and old pizzas. She would eat dry bread and uncooked crumpets, and lick any used plate that had been left on a kitchen surface. It was difficult to think of a cat who stole more food than she did, but Toby achieved that level of cat burglary expertise. Every single day he prowled round every corner of the kitchen and living room, eating the tiniest fragments. At one point, he attempted to eat a raw potato peeling and scoffed half a rasher of uncooked bacon.

There was no let up. I saw him leap on to the kitchen counter, pull a slice of bread out of its packaging and run off with it to eat behind the sofa. When I tried to take it off him, his ears went back and he crouched over it like it was prey, snarling at me. I chased him from the living room into Ronnie's downstairs bedroom to no avail. He sat under the bed, growling over his prize. Finally, I went back to the kitchen, got some of his dried cat food and swapped it for the bread.

Ronnie laughed. Toby was fulfilling his role as a therapy cat, cheering up Ronnie by his misbehaviour.

If I forgot to put the butter dish in the fridge, Toby would eat almost half the block, a quarter of a pound of butter. When I left a newly cooked semolina pudding out, he ate about a quarter of it, licking a hole in one side.

'If he lived under sharia law, he would have his paws cut off,' said Ronnie with obvious pride in *his* cat's villainy.

Toby's swag included a whole baked potato left on the kitchen worktop. I meant to keep all food out of reach but frequently forgot. He pushed the large potato on to the kitchen floor and ate half of it. When I left the recyling food bin open one morning, all the bones and skin of half a chicken were eaten – every single bone – plus a slice of very stale bread that I had thrown away.

After the chicken bones, I waited for the inevitable mess in the litter tray, but there was no bowel crisis. His motions were normal. Considering that he had been diagnosed as having a weak digestion, and that ordinary cat food upset his bowels, I could only think that he had spent a lot of his energy eating out of dustbins when he was a stray. He may have had a malabsorption problem with ordinary cat food but his digestion seemed perfectly adapted to scraps, bread, old toast, chicken bones and cold cooked potatoes. While other cats would have trouble digesting these items, Toby appeared invulnerable.

'You ought to feed him on scraps, rather than on the extremely expensive prescription food you're giving him,' Ronnie remarked, sagely.

Toby also seemed to thrive on porridge. Our breakfast consisted of porridge, with a handful of raisins. Toby had to be shut out of the kitchen while we ate because he would simply thrust his head into our bowls regardless of the fact that we were eating the porridge ourselves. As soon as we had finished we would let him into the kitchen and put down the bowls for him to lick. His weak digestion was fine with porridge, too.

Slowly he began to be willing to go out more. This was a relief. As he regained his energy, he had become very restless, pacing round and round the house, like a tiger in a zoo. Although I played with him as much as possible, he continued to chase Tilly on every occasion, clearly enjoying himself at her expense.

He also refused to use the scratching post, preferring the furniture. Cats often do, but I had the impression that Toby simply didn't know what a scratching post was. Perhaps he had never seen one before. He still had a lot to learn about living as a pet. I left little bits of food at its base, and rubbed catmint on it, to no avail. I could only hope that, if he ever did go out more, he would scratch on trees.

In February, he caught his first rodent. It wasn't a normal catch! Tilly had brought in a shrew and let it go in the living room. She had chased it up the curtain and it had dropped on Ronnie's bed, while he was taking his afternoon rest. Ronnie woke up suddenly to see a tiny form rushing towards him over the duvet. I would have screamed. Instead, Ronnie kept his head, swiped at it and it fell to the floor.

Toby shot across the room and caught it. He paraded round the room with the stiff-legged swagger that cats have when holding prey. I tried to usher him out. He dropped the poor little shrew a couple of times on the way, in the hall and kitchen, but at last he left the house.

Once he was outside, it became clear why he kept dropping it. He was holding the poor little thing by its backside, not by the neck. Inevitably, it doubled back and bit him on the chin. He dropped it, then grabbed it again by the backside. I don't think I had seen my other cats hold a rodent like that. All of them, even Ada, who at first did not know how to hunt, had carried their prey by the back of the neck. This method of holding prey was essential to avoid getting bitten.

Each time the shrew bit him, Toby flinched and swung his head so that the shrew flew through the air, landing about a yard away. Then he leapt over and picked it up again. It was obvious that he was not a skilled hunter. His expertise had been dustbins, not rodents.

I was pleased that his first real kill was a rodent and not a bird, because so far his only attempt at hunting had been trying to stalk the pheasants that came to the bird table. He was hopelessly maladroit about them, merely creeping on his stomach towards them in an obvious way. They would see him yards before he was anywhere near them and usually just stroll off, not even bothering to fly away.

Now he knew about rodents, perhaps he would go for them more than for birds. But his clumsiness in hunting amazed me. How come that, living rough, he didn't know about mice? Surely there must have been tasty mice on the estate where he hung out. This lack of skill was another reason for thinking that the vet might have been wrong about his age. Rather than two years old, I believed Toby to be only 18 months or even younger.

At times, I thought his sufferings might have affected his brain. Not only did he fail to hold a mouse properly by the nape of its neck, there were occasions when he seemed quite daft. I took both cats out into the garden on a sunny February day, and instead of investigating the long grass at the edge of the lawn, a haven for mice, he just ran up and down like a dog, looking overexcited and silly. His behaviour was so odd that I got the impression he didn't understand about proper cat patrolling.

I decided to take him further afield than the garden. I walked slowly a little way up the cart track to a piece of rough grass beyond the barn. Both cats followed. When Tilly arrived, she started looking around, scenting the smell of rabbits and investigating in a sensible feline way. Toby just ran around like an overexcited toddler. He ran away from me, turned and ran back. He bumped into my legs, then ran off again. He was behaving like a kitten, yet I had been told that he was fully adult.

When Gaynor came to give me my weekly exercise lessons, Toby recognized her and treated her as a familiar. He would roll on his back or rub against her. Did he know she was his saviour? I am sure he knew she was familiar to him but was he being grateful or just being an affection-mad creep? My cynicism about the feline species' capacity for gratitude made me favour the latter.

Sometimes he would try to take part in the lessons, taking up the space I needed on the exercise mat rather than watching from the armchair. His idea was to get close enough to me to touch me. This made exercise almost impossible so I would have to shut him out of the room altogether. During my training workout, Tilly stayed out of the room when he was around.

All in all, having Toby wasn't ideal for Tilly and I still had reservations about his permanence. While I appreciated his doglike devotion, it was not what I wanted; nor did I want a cat big enough to intimidate Tilly.

Yet Toby still needed me. It was possible he would never be completely healthy and that more vet's bills were on the way. My local cat rescue, Sunshine Cat Rescue, said they would take him but they could not possibly afford so costly a cat. It was also clear that Toby had loathed every moment of his time in the cattery pen. He had almost died trying to survive on the streets but being penned up stressed him in the extreme. With me, he was safe and happy.

I dithered. When I saw Tilly being chased, I felt he would have to go. When I looked at Toby's ginger body lying parallel to Ronnie's in the afternoons, and heard the cat snoring gently, I felt he would have to stay.

'Tilly would be much happier without him. Should I find him a home?' I asked Ronnie.

'Over my dead body,' he replied. Then he added sadly, 'Not even then, please.'

After that, Toby was here to stay.

Chapter 11

Training Toby and training myself

Death doesn't frighten cats. They are wiser than we are. They don't look forward to the unknown future and fear death. Like us, they suffer the aches of old age, the misery of illness, even the anxieties of an ageing brain and the pain of injury and wounds. Yet they don't ask themselves, 'Am I dying?' They have the gift of living in the present.

We can learn much from animals.

'The death rate for all of us is one hundred per cent,' Ronnie once remarked in the days when he was well and happy, travelling the world's trouble spots. He was sitting at his desk in the office we then shared in London, working on one of his terrorism books. He had the habit of making an occasional random remark out of nowhere. This one stuck in my mind.

He had seen dead bodies, first when he was a Royal Marine in World War Two, then when he was reporting on wars in the Middle East. 'A body isn't frightening,' he had reassured me when I was looking after my mother in the last year of her life. 'The person has gone.'

He was right, as I discovered when my mother died. Her body was no longer the person I had loved. It was just a body.

I had managed to sit with my mother for the terrible eight days it took her to die and that had taken its toll. For three months after her death I had been unable to go to sleep because of flashbacks that would come just before I lost consciousness. I used to have to keep reading until I fell into unconsciousness and the book literally fell from my hand, to avoid the torment of reliving those moments.

During five years of caring for Ronnie, seeing him through several near-death experiences, this fear of having to watch him die painfully and slowly in front of my eyes, like my mother, had haunted me. If I could take charge of his dying, I could make sure that he died an easy death, and did not have to go through the uncomfortable tortured death of my poor mother.

But could I take charge? Could I last out? Two years earlier I had had to wait for three weeks to know if my large amount of breast cancer was invasive or not. If it had been invasive, I reckoned I would have two years at the most. I would be ill from the treatment, and it would be touch and go whether I lived long enough to see Ronnie through his death first.

Fortunately, my cancer was pre-invasive and I had the strong probability of a normal lifespan, which meant I should outlive Ronnie, who was 18 years older than I am. Therefore I could hope to look after him right through his dying. In doing this, my darling cat Tilly helped most. Her recovery from stressed-out cat, unable to groom, to relaxed cat, taking care of herself, had inspired me to focus on *my* self-care. I had followed her example, as best I could.

As Ronnie had become more disabled by his cancers, I had worked out a timetable that included at least one two-hour walk a week, a rest almost every afternoon, and a week in each month for which I had a live-in carer. During that week, my days were free to do more walking, although I still had to do nighttime care.

Now the weight was rolling off me. I had never lost weight in my life. Through the years my weight had increased at the rate of about three ounces a year. As I stood on the scales, I felt a growing fear. Was the original breast cancer back, or did I have another cancer somewhere? I tried to argue myself into a more sensible frame of mind. I reminded myself that I'd had pre-invasive cancer and the chance of it returning to the tiny amount of breast tissue that remained was just two per cent.

Yet the fear wouldn't go away. There was a kind of superstitious logic to it. I believed, despite my better judgment, that caring for Ronnie had given me breast cancer in the first place, so continuing to care for him might give me another cancer. Perhaps I, too, had contracted lung cancer, from living with a pipe smoker for 40 years.

While I was waiting for the result of a chest X-ray, I obsessed about Toby. My mind, unlike the more sensible mind of a cat, would jump into an imagined future. Toby was still harassing Tilly and I was opening and shutting doors to keep them apart. In the imagined future, when I was trying to cope with cancer treatment myself *and* look after Ronnie, I didn't need cat difficulties.

We humans can torment ourselves so easily by living in the

future or, indeed, the past. I knew that I should live in the day, in the present moment, but I couldn't do it. My uncontrollable thoughts of a dire future told me that caring for Ronnie *was* killing me.

I lived in an imagined catastrophic future rather than in the present, and was tormented by an angry feeling of being trapped in a situation of my own choice. I loved Ronnie, but like a silent predatory beast, a fear of my own death, not his, stalked me. I woke to the fear in the morning and I lay down at night with the fear.

I considered joining a group of cancer survivors but the only one available was too far away. I could not get there and back in time to look after Ronnie. There was one at the local Maggie's Centre, a marvellous resource at the time when I was dealing with my cancer treatment.

A year or so earlier, I had been able to drop Ronnie at the hospital for his treatment and go to the centre for a cup of tea and a chat with the nurse there, before picking him up. Now Ronnie was too ill and too helpless. He needed me at his side at every hospital visit, to push his wheelchair, to cope with the appointments system, and to interpret between him and the doctors.

I was ashamed of my fear. I was ashamed of my anger. Many people give up their lives to care for their partners in old age without whingeing or complaining. I had no right to complain about my situation. I should just get on with it.

My fear and anger came mixed with self-pity, the most corrosive of all emotions and, for me, the most dangerous. Self-pity drives alcohol addicts back to drink. If I drank again, I would just walk out on Ronnie. I knew that. Drinking alcoholics are brutally selfish.

'All I want to do is to live long enough to have some fun. I would like to go to the opera. I would like to see friends. I would like to be able to walk in the dusk when and where I want to. I would like to be out of the house without worrying about getting back in time,' I wrote in the blog I kept at the time. 'I would like my freedom back.'

I blush with shame now when I read it. Ronnie was dying of cancer and I was complaining about not being able to go to the opera. Worse was to come. My worst moment came when I lost my temper with the helpless man that he had become. I have always had a temper that, once lost, is lost completely. I go into a shouting tantrum.

'What do you think it's like for me? I can't go out! I can't see friends! I can't go to the movies!' I ranted at him. When I managed to stop, the guilt and self-hatred were lacerating.

'How do you bear it when I do this?' I asked him, when apologizing for this outburst.

'You always have had a temper. I've got used to it.'

'But how do you deal with it? How can you bear me behaving like this?'

'I just don't listen,' he admitted. Once again, he had made me laugh.

'I don't feel I'm with the wrong woman,' he said, reassuringly. 'But I do feel bad about you. I feel guilty and sad. We were so happy … but I'm so grateful that you're here.'

I look back and thank God that this temper tantrum was the last. When I remember that conversation, I can see the sheer exhaustion and stress that lay behind my unkind behaviour. At least it prompted me to try to do something about my self-inflicted tormenting thoughts. In particular, I needed to take

191

some action about the self-pity. For a large part of my life, some of my special friends had suggested I write gratitude lists when the self-pity kicked in. I had never done so. To write a list of the good things in my life sounded like a platitudinous suggestion in a Victorian children's book – puerile, creepy and unpleasantly pious. Now I really, really needed them. In desperation, I wrote my first one.

- *I have survived cancer. I have a 98 per cent chance of a full lifespan. I must always remember this. I have been given a third chance – life after cancer, a gift this time like the emotional and spiritual second life I was given when I stopped drinking.*
- *Ronnie is still with me. I love him. When I am overwhelmed with exhaustion and frustration, I don't always appreciate him. Indeed, there are times when I wish he wasn't still here. But overall, I am very, very, very glad he is still with me.*
- *I have two wonderful cats.*
- *Toby and Tilly are not friends but they are not enemies either. There have been no fights.*
- *I have enough money to pay for help from carers.*
- *I am beginning to regain some fitness. When I have a live-in carer, I have walked for an hour about four days out of seven and the improvement is showing.*
- *I have a warm house and a loving partner.*
- *I have lost a lot of weight so my figure looks great.*

The list worked. It wasn't so much the detail of what it said; just writing it turned my mind in a better direction. I still felt fear, and some anger, but the gratitude list gave me relief from the self-pity. Compared with many people, I had a great life.

Plenty of people were far worse off than I was. I made a similar list about two or three times a week, just to get the emotional relief. The gratitude list was a great mental tool.

Sometimes the list had just one or two very small things on it, like this one.

- *Toby is outside this morning: he is learning to live again.*
- *Tilly purred so loudly last night that I fell asleep to the rhythm of that purr.*
- *My local library has got two huge books for me on inter-library loan. They would have cost me about £250 to buy.*
- *The car park opposite is free for three hours and I can do the trip for the books in less than an hour, which means I can do it any afternoon.*
- *I made a really good moussaka. Harder work than I had thought. This made up for the cheese straw disasters.*
- *I am able to go to the Lent discussion group, even though I have to leave early. It is helping me remember the spiritual side of life. I am more than a body and a brain.*

Even this list of small things helped. Just as Ronnie had come to value the small kindnesses in an ordinary day, so I came to value the small blessings of an ordinary day. His attitude had shown me what to do.

True, there was much that was unpleasant about being a carer, mostly to do with toileting, the cleaning up and the smells, and much that was heart-rending – the way he looked so ill and the way if I so much as brushed against him he yelped with pain.

In my family, illness was a disgrace, not a misfortune. My father could not bear ill people and took the view that all illness should be ignored. I don't know if he ever visited friends in hospital. I know that, after a stroke, he wouldn't let people visit *him* in hospital because he didn't want them to see him in his weakness. My mother also wouldn't visit ill people in hospital, particularly those with cancer, a disease that had killed her sister. She was too frightened to be near anybody who was seriously ill.

In this fear of illness, many animals are not so different. Animals sometimes avoid or occasionally even attack others that are ill. Healthy hens will peck a sick hen to death, for instance. Those friends who could not bear to visit Ronnie were showing a natural behaviour. After all, avoiding sick people was probably evolution's way of making us less likely to catch infections. Those who avoided sick people might live longer. That thought helped me feel better about those who shunned us.

It also helped me to forgive myself for my intermittent disgust during caring. I just had to override that natural feeling. To do that, I would sometimes list Ronnie's continuing good points. One such list went:

- *I love the way he rises to the occasion when visitors turn up. He is at his best with others, not me, which is natural and good.*
- *He never ever complains. He is very brave.*
- *He stays pleasant almost all the time. The most he ever does, if I lose my temper or some new misfortune happens, might be to cry. Silently because he knows that his crying upsets me. He tries his best to look after me in any way he can.*
- *He still enjoys a joke. And even occasionally makes one. If I could stop comparing him to the man he once was, I would see more good in him. I keep seeing the loss rather than what remains.*

The lists helped, and so did living down a cart track surrounded by fields. I could take little walks down the track, leaving Ronnie for about half an hour or so. Nature was all around me.

In the snow that fell after Christmas, despite not feeling too good, I walked down the cart track, leaving footsteps about six or seven inches deep. I sometimes found myself stepping on ice, and my feet would break through to the puddle of water beneath. Sometimes I sank into mud below the snow, leaving a stain of brown at the bottom of my footprint; sometimes my step landed on the frozen grass showing the green below the white.

The wind had whipped the snow deep in some places, leaving bare, frozen earth in others. The wind and snow were sharp on my face. Every now and again a snowflake reached my mouth and burst on my tongue like a champagne bubble. The leaves had fallen off most of the hedges, but the occasional red hawthorn berry remained, so far uneaten by blackbirds or pigeons. Leaves were still there on the brambles, some low enough for small animals, such as rabbits, to browse.

Wildlife had retreated from fields to hedges. A blackbird pecked at the foot of a hedge. Pheasants and French partridges searched for food there. The whirr of 14 pairs of wings cut through the snowy silence as the partridges flew away. One was left behind. His wing must have been broken by shot. He somehow ran and fluttered into the shelter of the hedge. The *chuk chuk* call of a pheasant was one of the few bird sounds I could hear. Silence had settled with the snow.

Then came a moment of magic. A hare started up halfway down the field to the left of the track. She must have seen my outline moving against the snow. She ran down parallel to the hedge, still in the deep, powdery snow, then through the gateway and across the stubble that had been left for set-aside, where the wind had swept some of the snow away. As she ran, her hind legs threw up a flurry of snow and I had a few moments of perfect peace.

I had taken that short walk and experienced that moment of transcendence because I was nearly housebound.

Hares were, and are, special for me, but they were not always visible. Not every walk down the track produced that miracle moment. When the hillside was windy and cold, they stayed in the valley below. But I often walked down the track in the hope of seeing them, even at a distance. When I reached the gateway at the end, I would look out cautiously just in case a hare was nearby. They could not see me if I was in the shadow of the hedge and if all my movements were very, very slow.

On one evening, when I was standing motionless by the gate at the end of the track, quite far from the house, I saw a small brown figure, Tilly, walking towards me from the other side of the field. She had never come that far before. Indeed, few of my cats had ventured that long distance from the house. Yet there she was, intent on joining me.

When she reached me, she did a silent miaow – mouth open with no sound – and rubbed against my legs. I thought she looked anxious. Then she turned and started for home. After about two feet, she stopped and looked back. It was clear she wanted me to follow her. So instead of staying where I was, which I would have liked to do, I followed her home. Every three feet or so she paused to make sure I was following. She had come far out of her safe territory to rescue me and to take me home. It was very touching.

Toby, in the meantime, was getting more confident every day, and he decided he would upgrade his food. Although he continued to steal any crumb left on the kitchen floor, he started refusing to eat all of his specialist diet. The starving stray was now turning up his nose at an excellent dinner!

Like most cats, he was trying to train me to give him a different diet, preferably the most expensive cat food in the supermarket; or perhaps he had in mind a dustbin diet, made up of discarded human food, which apparently suited his otherwise oversensitive gut. I would have given in and changed him over to ordinary cat food, except that I knew it would be bad for his digestion. The litter tray would suffer and I was the one who had to clean it.

Luckily, I had a gannet cat at hand – Tilly. I dealt with Toby's reluctance to eat by handing the half finished bowl to Tilly, who scoffed the lot in front of his eyes. After three such experiences, he gobbled it up, anxious that she should not get it. He gave up trying to persuade me to change his diet, and reverted to his ordinary greedy pig behaviour with the special food.

When somebody sent me a food dispenser for dogs, both cats were ideal testers of the device. The idea was to see if it worked for cats. The device was made of green plastic with upstanding prongs, and the cat had to hook up dry food from between them. A food dispenser like this one should make eating more satisfying for indoor cats who don't have enough to do; and for a cat such as Tilly, who gobbled up everything too fast, it should slow down food intake so that the cat felt fuller quicker and (hopefully) would eat less.

No such luck. Perhaps because she was a tiny cat, she

hooked out her daily portion of dried food in double-quick time and immediately looked for more. She was only a tad slower than she would have been if the food had been put into a bowl.

Toby, on the other hand, appeared unable to understand what he should do with the device. Despite being as greedy as Tilly, he simply looked at it and walked away when I planted his special dry food in it. When I put bits of old bread in it (usually irresistible to a cat addicted to dustbin food) he continued to ignore it. Was he so cross-eyed that he couldn't see it? There were moments when I wondered whether life on the streets had impaired his ability to think. (Cats *do* think, even if they don't think like we do.) Was he brain damaged or just stupid?

Emotionally, if not brain-wise, he was improving. He had stopped pacing round the house like a caged mini ginger lion. He would now go into the garden even if there were no breadcrumbs under the bird table. He was still overdependent on me, but he was getting a bit less clinging.

On the rare days when Toby decided to rest with me instead of Ronnie, he would sit very close to my head, as I lay on the sofa, aligning his body so it touched mine at all points. From this position he would often wash himself very vigorously and noisily, disrupting the afternoon nap I so badly needed.

Later, as he became less emotionally dependent on me, he no longer had to sleep touching me. He was content to lie on one of the armchairs while I was on the sofa. If I called his name to get his attention, he would occasionally give me that well-known feline look of contempt that says, 'No way am I going to bother responding.' This was a sign of his recovery!

Normally, that refusal to pay attention when called would not matter much in a cat but I needed to call him off Tilly. I consulted my friend Beverley Saucell of Fetch!, an expert in dog behaviour, who suggested clicker training Toby, that is using a small device that makes a click sound, which tells the animal that it has performed the right action and a food reward will follow shortly. I had done this with Tilly, who as a result could perform charming, if useless, tricks, such as sitting on command, begging, shaking hands and jumping over an object. Toby, on the other hand, would be trained for something useful. The aim was for me to call him off chasing Tilly by training him to come and touch my hand on command. As he was as greedy as Tilly, I thought he would be easy to motivate.

Another behaviourist friend, Dr Sarah Millsopp, suggested I try the voice equivalent of the clicker, so that I could use the method to call Toby even when I didn't have a clicker to hand. I chose 'beep beep' as my voice equivalent, because those two words are not used in normal conversation. Using everyday words might easily confuse the animal being trained.

Also, I didn't want the two cats to get muddled. If I used a clicker for both cats, Tilly might think the clicker noise applied to her when it was aimed at Toby. Good dog trainers never worry about this but I am not a very good trainer, having never attended clicker-training classes, as I should have done. So I didn't have confidence in my ability to train two different cats with the same clicker noise.

If Toby really was brain damaged, my training might not work. I started by simply teaching him that 'beep beep' meant food was coming within a very few seconds. 'Beep beep,' I would say, then hand him a cat biscuit. I fed him this way for about three days – not his wet-food portion in the morning, but his dry-food portion later in the day.

The next stage was target training. By training an animal to follow a target, you can move it around as you choose. I chose a dog's training target – a collapsible wand with a large red bulb at the end.

The advantage of target training was twofold. It meant I didn't have to do too much luring with food, that is showing the food to the animal in advance so that it pays attention to your hand. There's nothing wrong with this as a training method but it relies on food being in the hand at all times. I had taught Tilly to do little tricks using a clicker but any good dog trainer would have told me that I was doing too much luring her into position by showing her the food. I also had a bad habit of unconsciously moving my arms about, so that she followed these movements rather than the verbal command that accompanied them. If I had to hold a target, I wouldn't be able to do the distracting arm movements.

Naturally, at first Toby couldn't see the point of what I was trying to do. So I divided his lunch into small handfuls of dried food and used them to reward him when he did the right thing. I rewarded him with a cat biscuit first of all when he just looked at the target, then, again, if he moved even a little way towards it. By the end of five or six minutes, it seemed as though he might have a glimmer of an idea about the process. Each time he went nearer the red bulb, I said, 'Beep beep,' and gave him the food.

At teatime I followed the same procedure, less successfully because Tilly got into the room and Toby was distracted when I threw her some food to keep her away. However, after I had removed her, I think he was beginning to realize that he got food when he was near the target.

He looked up at me, I gazed at the target and he followed my gaze. Cats can follow the human gaze and Toby was very attached to me, so he was happy to look where my gaze was pointing.

This time, he was rewarded only when he was within two inches of the target. I didn't use any verbal commands, or cues, since I had read it is best to add these later on in training. Two days later, he was going up close to the target and being rewarded with the 'beep beep' noise followed by food.

He didn't seem keen to touch the target directly with his nose. This may have been because cats don't nose around as much as dogs do. Dogs are happy to push balls with their noses. So I decided it would be good enough if he put his nose very close without actually touching. The next stage was to put in the verbal command, 'Touch.'

It wasn't too difficult. The 'touch' command was to tell him what I wanted him to do. The 'beep beep' was to tell him that he had successfully done it and that I would give him some food very soon. He caught on fast for a cat that had appeared to be brain damaged. Once he had learned what to do, I made the target my own hand in case I didn't have the wand with the red bulb with me when I wanted him to come and leave Tilly alone.

I also sometimes rewarded him with lots of cat biscuits and sometimes none at all. This is how fruit machines work, randomly giving no rewards then giving occasional jackpots. It's well known that people continue to play fruit machines for hours on this system. If they got a small reward of a few pence at regular intervals, instead of a jackpot very occasionally, they wouldn't bother to play for so long. So giving Toby an occasional jackpot of many cat biscuits was a great way to keep him interested in touching my hand on command.

So far so good. I discovered, however, that I could not call him off once he had started the chase. I could divert him if he was just looking and thinking about it, but once he started moving, it was too late. What made it worse was that Tilly would often run before he chased her, and once she had started running, he would entirely ignore my command of, 'Touch.'

After chasing her, he would come to the command willingly and promptly but once the chase was on, he was unable to focus on me at all. Luckily, I noticed that, beforehand, he would often give her a hard predatory stare and lower his head. If I saw this body language in time, I could call him off.

To worry about my cats' welfare while my husband was getting more and more ill may seem hard-hearted. But I could do nothing for Ronnie now, except look after him and, so far as was possible, help him keep his dignity. Worrying about my cats was better than dwelling on my fears.

Occasionally, encouraging moments occurred between the cats. I looked out one morning when Toby had gone into the garden with Tilly. He chased her into the bushes then sauntered off towards the vegetable patch, where he no doubt planned to dig and defecate in my seedbed. Tilly ran after him and chased him up the oak tree.

The cats were working out their relationship. Now I had to work out how to fix myself. My tests had come back clear from cancer, but with raised inflammation bodies, a sign either of some future illness or of the past virus. I did not have cancer but nonetheless I could not go on living a life filled with self-inflicted feelings of frustration, self-pity and fear, and subsequently shame.

'I'm not sure how long I can go on doing this,' I said to Ronnie.

'I don't think it will be very long now,' he replied.

I feel remorse every time I remember that conversation. I could not change the fact that he was ill and dying. I could not change the uncertainty of how long he had left to live, perhaps days, perhaps years. I wish now that I had not made that remark.

My self-pity and fear for myself arose from living with the worry of an uncertain future. My cats just accepted things as they were. I needed to learn a lesson from my cats.

Chapter 12

The Last days with Ronnie

'Darling Tilly,' I murmured during the night. 'What am I going to do?' She purred quietly back as she lay on the bed.

'Toby, what do you think?' I asked him the next morning as he scuttled round, looking for crumbs on the kitchen floor.

I talk to my cats. Don't we all? The wonderful thing about this one-way conversation is that cats never talk back. They don't make suggestions. They don't tell you what to do. They just listen to what you say and then get on with their own lives. It's like talking to a good therapist. You can say anything you like to them.

Talking to the cats helped, but I needed some thinking time.

I found day and nighttime carers for Ronnie and set off for four days walking on the rain- and mist-shrouded moors of Exmoor in the West Country, in all their remoteness and beauty. It was my first long break for two years, and I came home rested and relaxed.

Best of all, the struggle with fear and shame in my mind had left me. As I drove back home down the motorway, I *knew* that I would not let Ronnie go to a nursing home, whatever the cost to me. He would die at home where I could look after him and be with him. Even if it killed me, I would look after him and give him as good a death as I could.

The decision taken, my mind cleared. I no longer had to worry about the future. I could live with things as they were, not as they might be. Acceptance really was the answer to my situation.

Ronnie had always been better than I am at accepting things as they were. It was one of the reasons why I loved him. Years earlier, before the arrival of Toby and around the time when he was first diagnosed with prostate cancer, we had gone to visit my friend Sacha. She had been diagnosed with advanced pancreatic cancer about the same time. Ronnie had been told that he had two years to live. Sacha had been told there would be no more treatment. Both were, I think, still in shock.

I could tell my presence was preventing them talking honestly to each other, so I found an excuse to leave them together in her little house in Wales. Later, I asked Ronnie what they had talked about. 'I told her to take courage. We all have to die,' he said.

He wouldn't tell me any more about that conversation but later he explained how he had dealt with his *own* diagnosis. 'I was only shocked for the first few weeks,' he said. 'Then in my optimistic way I accepted it. Acceptance is the key. It wasn't the worst part of my life.'

He added, 'I'm not sitting here thinking spiritual thoughts about it. I'm not interested in last-minute deathbed conversions. I know I'm near the end of the road. I'm not frightened of dying. I'm ready for it.'

Ronnie was just a little bit weaker when I got back home. I had, of course, rung him every day to check that he was all right. He had not minded too much being in other people's care, because he was still in his own house. One carer had looked after him at night, the other during the day. Both told me that they had found it exhausting, getting up through the night – helpful comments that made me feel better about taking some time off.

Strangely, it was Toby who had suffered a relapse. The first evening I was back he sat very close to me on the sofa and it was like sitting near a blocked drain. For two hours he released the most awful-smelling wind, so much so that one of the daily carers, who was less keen on cats than I was, nicknamed him 'Stinker'. I found that hurtful, even though Toby didn't care a fig about it.

Then the day after my arrival home, he was sick. There was no sign of hairballs. Had he eaten a bumble bee or a beetle, or found some mouldy food remnants? I didn't notice anything missing in the kitchen. Normally, when he stole food, he did not suffer from wind, being digestively adapted to the stray-cat dustbin diet.

I took Toby to the vet later on in the day because after being sick he refused to eat his normal food. For Toby to refuse food, it must have been serious. He simpered and raised his head for a scratch while on the vet's table. He sat without a struggle on the weighing machine, looking elegant and handsome, relatively at ease in the surgery and very anxious to solicit stroking from the vet. Toby had a high level of people skills.

'Give him some plain chicken to eat,' said the vet. 'Bring him back over the weekend if he won't eat it. I'll see him again next week.'

So Toby ate the meat off a cold chicken leg I was going to have for my supper that night. He ate with relish but still refused his own food. I decided he did not need emergency vet care if he was able to eat cold chicken. Over the weekend he started eating his own food again and the litter tray confirmed that his digestive crisis was over. I took him back to the vet that Monday to confirm his recovery and paid yet another bill!

I could have flattered myself that his digestive disturbance was due to missing me, but his calm attitude towards my return did not suggest he had been unduly disturbed by my absence. It remained a mystery.

These intermittent health problems confirmed our earlier decision to keep Toby in my care. Now I had two reasons to keep him. The first and most important reason was that Ronnie wanted him to stay, and he was performing his duties as Ronnie's feline companion. The second reason was that Toby himself needed an owner who had the resources to afford a steady contribution to the local vet! Toby was an earning opportunity for my vet.

The first warm morning of the spring brought new hope that the cats were accepting each other. They went out from the kitchen door together and I saw them both in the shelter of the open garden shed. Toby was just sitting and Tilly was rolling on the concrete – not lying on one side with all four paws and claws ready to attack, but rolling in a social way. If she had been terrified of Toby, she would not have dared to behave in that way.

Alone together they were fine. The stress point in their relationship was me. If I was around, Toby pushed her out of the way to make sure he had me to himself. He was a mummy's cat who wouldn't share. There was only one of me, and Ronnie, although an agreeable sleeping companion in the afternoons, was still no substitute in Toby's eyes.

I had hopes that Toby was becoming a little more independent. Two months earlier I had picked him up and taken him to bed with me one afternoon and put him under the covers, with his head poking out. He seemed happy with this arrangement. I do not think he really enjoyed it much but he would put up with this kind of human behaviour just to be near me. Now he was becoming distinctly less cuddly. He did not, thank you very much, want to be under the bed covers ever again. He was definite, too, that he would not spend time on my lap – resting touching me was fine, lying on my lap was not.

In every way he became less compliant. I could pick him up and put him on a chair and he would immediately leave, making it clear that whichever chair he sat on was his choice, not mine. His behaviour began to show a proper feline contempt for mere humans!

He still competed with Tilly for my attention, driving her away from me with a gentle push if she got too close. I would have to timeshare myself, not just at night but during the day. I decided that Tilly was the cat who should be allowed on my office desk. She had her heated bed there in winter and a mat in summer. Toby was allowed on the floor in my office.

I never punished him or even touched him if he got on the desk. Each time he jumped up, I got up and left the room. Then he would jump down from the desk and leave the room with me. He was learning that if he jumped on the desk, I would leave the office. When he stayed on the office floor, I would pet him, but not otherwise.

In one thing, and one thing only, did Toby no longer compete with Tilly, and allow me to decide his movements. Each afternoon I would put Toby in Ronnie's room to sleep on his bed. He would stay there while Tilly and I slept on the sofa.

Soon after my return from Exmoor, Ronnie said, 'I think it's time we sold my car.'

My first reaction was relief. We had two cars outside our house – mine, a small, dirty Skoda, and Ronnie's, a larger, more dashing Saab. The Saab was easier for Ronnie to access but since Christmas he had been too weak to walk to any car, needing his wheelchair and a special wheelchair taxi for any hospital appointment.

Besides, he had decided that he did not wish to go to any more hospital appointments. There was little, if anything, the cancer team could do for him. So the car was sitting doing nothing and costing a fortune in insurance and tax. I had not talked to him about this waste of money, because I knew that the car mattered to him. It was more than a car.

Deciding that we should sell the car meant he was preparing himself for death. To him, the car had been a symbol of his strength, his status as a man and his independence. Now he was bidding farewell to all those things and, because he knew I was hopeless with cars, he was taking from me the burden of disposing of it later.

Although from the outside it looked as if I was the carer and he the person being cared for, he was still caring for me.

So the car went and the warmer weather of early summer came. Ronnie managed to walk out of the back door and have tea with friends in the garden, but the effort exhausted him so much he couldn't really follow the conversation.

In the warm weather, Toby strolled out and started to treat the garden as if it was his territory. He would pause and spray in the same areas where William had sprayed. He patrolled the garden. He now had outside interests and hobbies, so he chased Tilly less frequently.

Tilly was also out a lot. In the evening, when I took a short walk down the track to the fields, she would come with me. One evening, a very young hare, a leveret with a baby face, ran up to within four feet of both of us. For me, she was a messenger of acceptance, of joy and awe at the gift of the world. It was like a promise that I could still be happy despite what was happening to Ronnie. So were the house martins that started nesting in my porch. The year before, two youngsters had sheltered there at the end of the summer, and now they had returned to make a nest. Some kind of serenity came into my life.

Toby also became more serene. He became more himself and it was clear that he was a bit of a feline eccentric. He had a habit of peeing in rabbit or rat holes – and there were plenty of those in my garden and the nearby field. He would simply squat and deliver a jet of urine down them.

He also preferred to poo in the long grass, rather than on the loose earth of my vegetable garden, a preference I was keen to encourage. When he was happy, he would rush around, leaping in the air. When he felt lonely, he would pause and make a series of long, yowling miaows, as if he was still a proper tomcat, not a neutered male. And he always greeted me, not with the traditional cat chirrup, but with a series of small kitten cries.

It seemed he had a reasonable IQ. He might not have been the brightest kitten in the basket, but perhaps when he first arrived, he had been so ill or stressed that he could not think properly. I realized he had a brain when I rescued a very small shrew.

Over the years I have rescued scores of mice and shrews by putting down a Wellington boot and sweeping them into it, then putting the boot on its side in the hedge and waiting for the rescued rodent to emerge. None of my cats – Fat Ada, Little Mog, George, William or Tilly – had ever managed to work out what I was doing. They would show no interest in the boot that contained the mouse, as if they did not realize it was there. They would wander round, looking confused, while the mouse emerged safely from the boot.

Not so Toby. He was able to understand that the mouse had not disappeared altogether. It was inside the boot. This particular occasion started when he proudly brought the tiny shrew into the kitchen, trailed by a hopeful Tilly, from whom he may well have stolen it in the first place. He played with it in the kitchen while I went to get the boot. The rescue was more difficult than usual, due to his interference. He pulled the shrew back from the boot a couple of times.

Finally, I swept it in with a twig and put the boot in the hedge. Toby hung about the place where he had last seen it, looking cross. I went back to my cooking. When I looked out, Toby had the shrew again.

How had he done this? Had he sneaked off to the hedge and met his prey by sheer chance after it had emerged from the boot? I thought not. I believed that, unlike the other cats, he had realized the mouse was inside the boot. Perhaps he had hooked his paw into the boot and pulled the cowering rodent out. More likely, he had waited nearby and ambushed it as it emerged. He wasn't as dim as he sometimes appeared to be.

He showed signs of intelligence, too, when he was shut away in his room in the evening with his cat biscuits. One night he suddenly appeared downstairs, to the consternation of Tilly, who was relaxing away from his presence.

Had he learned to open the door? No. The door was still closed. Then I remembered I had opened the window to reduce the smell of cat in the room. He must have jumped from the first-floor window on to the hard track and come in through the cat flap. Later, he did discover that, if I had not closed the door securely, he could open it by flinging himself against it.

While Toby was getting stronger, Ronnie was getting weaker. I could measure his decline by his consumption of bacon and eggs. He was finding it ever more difficult to eat. Every single day for the past two years he had enjoyed bacon and eggs in the evening. Now he struggled to eat this meal. From two eggs and two rashers, he was down to one egg and a single rasher.

So often, people try to 'fight' cancer on behalf of their loved ones, and cancer sufferers also see their illness as something to struggle against. Ronnie, who had seen some real fighting in World War Two, and had reported on about 30 or so wars or small military actions, always disliked the military metaphor for illness. 'I am definitely not fighting cancer,' he had declared.

I'd had that attitude of trying to fight cancer when my mother had fallen ill. When I failed, and she died, it felt like a defeat, not just a bereavement. I said to Ronnie, 'All my efforts have been wasted.'

'They were not wasted, Celia. By your efforts you showed her how much you loved her,' he replied.

So now I knew what I was doing. I wasn't fighting to keep Ronnie alive. My mission was to make him happy, pain free and comfortable rather than search for miracle treatments.

I realized that he had weeks not months to live when, one morning, he could no longer walk to the breakfast table in the kitchen. He was able to move from his bed to his living-room chair and, after being washed by the carers in the chair, he ate his breakfast there. He had rallied before when nobody expected him to, though, so perhaps this time he would pull himself back from the brink of death.

When I measured his oxygen levels, they were much lower than they had ever been before. Two years earlier I would have rung the doctor's surgery or the ambulance on his behalf, but now I was anxious to keep him out of hospital. I didn't want him to die in a busy geriatric ward.

I phoned Lizzie, the palliative nurse. She promised to visit that very morning. With the wisdom of her calling, she said to me, 'There's no point in him going to hospital unless there's something they can do for him.'

She suggested getting him oxygen and a hoist so that if he took to his bed, we could move him to wash him. A home visit from a respiratory team and a visit from the occupational therapist were booked for the next day. That night he refused bacon and eggs in favour of a cup of Complan.

The next morning he managed to walk to his chair with the aid of his morning carers but he ate just half of his porridge. I did not press him to finish it. When I looked in at him in his chair half an hour later, he was shaking and incoherent. He was staring into midair and did not speak to me.

'Who is the prime minister?' I asked him. He stayed silent.

'What was your father's first name?' I asked.

'Richard,' he mumbled.

I took his oxygen level again and it had plunged by a third lower than it should have been. I rang Lizzie in a panic and said, 'I don't know what to do.' She promised to visit that morning. Then, when Ronnie was trying to stand up to have a pee, he toppled back. He lay stranded half on and half off the chair, white faced and with an expression that said, 'Help me.'

All I could do was adjust the chair so that it supported his legs, and stuff pillows around him to support his body. I had to ring the ambulance, because I could not singlehanded get him back into the chair. I sat nearby holding his hand. I could see he was uncomfortable and perhaps in pain but he said nothing.

Now I could do nothing more for him except be near him.

Two ambulance men arrived and helped him back onto his chair. He refused to be put into his bed. 'Put me in the chair,' he ordered. He was not ready to give up.

'We must take you to hospital,' said one of the paramedics.

Ronnie shook his head firmly in refusal. So I said, 'I do not give you permission to move him. Nor does he.' They were following the correct protocols, but hospital was not where Ronnie wanted to be.

Then it seemed as if the house became crowded. The community nurse arrived for her normal visit, which I had

215

forgotten. Lizzie, the palliative nurse, arrived, too, and organized home nursing for nights, and oxygen. A respiratory nurse came and signed for oxygen. A smart girl in a uniform came up the track in a van and installed an oxygen tank with a mask. The doctor turned up and signed the essential pink forms, which meant Ronnie could have a morphine driver, a gadget that allows the painkiller to enter the body directly, under the skin, at regular intervals.

This wasn't the cruel Liverpool Care Pathway that had been so ineffectual and brought about the lingering death of my mother by starvation and dehydration. Whether Ronnie died or lived was not discussed at all. The oxygen and the morphine were there to relieve pain or discomfort. If they hastened or delayed his death, it was irrelevant.

Then Ronnie, who had travelled to wars throughout the world from Vietnam to the Middle East, made his last journey – ten yards from the living room to his bedroom. He needed the help of two occupational therapists, who had come to install a hoist that he would no longer need. Supported by them, he walked from his chair to his bed. Those ten yards were the hardest journey of his life. Somehow he managed them.

That afternoon he slept, an ordinary good sleep. The oxygen brought colour to his cheeks and the morphine reduced his pain. He looked comfortable. I dared not let Toby sleep on his bed as he normally would have done. Ronnie was so frail that I feared even Toby's four kilos of weight might cause him pain. I had to shut him away in the hall and the kitchen, indignant though he was.

For me, even the living room, only ten yards away from his bed, was too far away from him now. I needed to be in the same room. I moved an armchair into his bedroom and immediately Tilly jumped onto it. This seemed right somehow. It was safe to have her nearby as she had always refused to sit on his bed.

So I brought my duvet into his bedroom and lay on the floor between his bed and the armchair where Tilly was now sound asleep. I needed to be physically and emotionally close to him. There was no sound except for the oxygen machine, which puffed like an old-fashioned steam engine. I also fell asleep.

About an hour later, Lizzie and Penelope came back with a drugs box and put the morphine driver into his arm. Carers, known as 'the hospital at home team', were organized to visit three times a day. By a happy chance, they came from the same agency as those who normally came in the mornings. They were, therefore, women he already knew and liked.

He recognized them and smiled. Caring for him involved moving him and it was clear that every part of his body hurt. He wore what I had always thought of as his Royal Marine expression. Making no complaint or sound, his face said, 'I will bear this.'

Brian, a friend and a clergyman, came to see him and I left them alone in case Ronnie needed to talk about something without my being there. Ronnie had said to me a few months earlier that he partly believed in God. 'I don't believe in life after death and that's a good thing really. It's one less thing to worry about.'

His father had been a Primitive Methodist minister and his mother had died young. Ronnie had added, 'At home, we believed in a kindly God. My father always spoke about a homeland. He believed he would meet my mother, Nellie, again. He certainly hoped so. So I have a certain hope.'

Others came to say goodbye to him – my nephew and niece, his stepdaughter, Helen, and other friends. He was well enough to recognize and be pleased with people who visited. That evening, before the night nurse came, I was sitting in a chair near him when he made some kind of noise – not a groan exactly, but a sound asking for help.

'Are you cold?' I asked him.

'Yes.' He could still speak. Just.

'Would you like something to drink?' I asked.

'Yes,' he was able to reply.

I held a bottle of mineral water to his lips and tipped it for him to take little sips, pausing between each sip for him to swallow, which sometimes meant a longish pause. Occasionally, he would cough a little after swallowing. Then I would put the oxygen mask back on him for three or four breaths, before giving him more.

He'd said he was cold, so I put a warm Indian woollen shawl over his body below the duvet. I had to be careful about holding his hand. I just let it rest on mine because if I put the slightest pressure on it, I could tell from his expression that it was painful.

Then he suddenly said, 'Not Morse.' Then again, urgently, 'Not Morse.' Did he mean *Morse* the TV series or, 'Not more.'

'No Morse. No more,' I said. Then I said it firmly and reassuringly a second time, adding, 'Don't worry. I'm looking after you.'

About an hour later he seemed to be hot and distressed. I took off the duvet so that he just had the Indian shawl over him. He wanted his top off (he was wearing a long-sleeved polo shirt) but I waited for the night nurse to take that off. I feared that the slightest touch would be too painful.

'I want the details,' he said, urgently and suddenly. 'I must have the details.'

I wondered if his mind was in some other place, perhaps asking a journalist's question of some foreign general. But at least I could give him some kind of answer. So I told him details of the oxygen, telling him about the pretty girl who had delivered and set up the equipment, and how it worked. And with this detailed answer he seemed content. If in his mind this was his last journalistic assignment, he had been given the information he wanted.

He drank a little more water. I put water on a cotton swab and wiped it on his brow, his cheeks and his eyes to cool him down. I could see he liked this.

Sometimes his body shook. I wasn't sure if he was hot or if he was cold but I put the duvet back on. I was glad when Sue the night nurse turned up and I could leave him to her expert care. Ronnie and she decided he would enjoy a whisky sour. She found some orange barley water and laced it with a little Scotch so that he enjoyed the deathbed equivalent of the Cyprus whisky sours we had both enjoyed when we first ran off together.

In the early hours of the morning I woke from upstairs where I was sleeping to hear him shout something. Sue was sitting with him during the night but I felt he needed me. So I went down.

'Were you having a bad dream?' I asked.

'It was more than that. It was much more than that,' he said insistently.

'I love you. You are all right. I'm here,' I said. My presence seemed to calm him.

Sue said that morphine could make people agitated, so she gave him a tranquilizer injection before leaving. That morning, the nursing agency rang to apologize that they could not send anybody during the day, but I was pleased to be alone with him. We had so little time left.

His eyelids were now partially open. He could move his hands a little but otherwise he lay rigid. He could still recognize me but his breathing was crackling and croaky. He did not struggle or fight to draw in more oxygen. He was calm. Perhaps the tranquilizing injection was working, or, more likely, he was calm because he had accepted his death and was not fighting to stay alive.

His only discomfort occurred when he peed. I would lean over him and say to him, 'It's all right. You can pee in the knickers. That's what they're for.' And he would recognize my voice and calm down again. I was glad I was there. He was not surrounded by strangers. He still shook occasionally, and occasionally he would take two sips of water and shake his head to show he did not want more.

Brian came and this time I stayed in the room while he said two prayers. Ronnie could no longer speak. Could he hear me as I leant over his bed and told him I loved him? I was not sure. He was further on his journey, passing through that boundary that separates life from death.

I put on some Handel, music that I would like to hear when I am dying. Various people visited. Their company was cheering for me, even though by now Ronnie may not have known if they were there.

In the afternoon, a community nurse came to renew the morphine and the tranquilizer in the driver. Ronnie had become even less responsive. His eyes were still half open rather than closed. His mouth had fallen open. I was not sure if he knew me. His body was closing down and it was as if his mind was intent on something else. I was losing sense of time. He and I were outside time. Being together was timeless.

My mother had laboured to breathe. Ronnie's breathing was unhurried, without effort, regular though weak. He was not struggling to live. In the afternoon, Toby jumped onto his bed near his legs before I could stop him. Ronnie did not respond. Toby had been wanting to do this all day and I had stopped him in case his weight hurt Ronnie. But Toby, as if he knew that Ronnie was not sleeping but dying, stayed only a minute and then jumped down.

I have wondered if Toby came to investigate what was going on. Did he miss the drowsy, welcoming response that usually greeted his arrival to sleep with Ronnie in the afternoons? Animals may well recognize dying; perhaps Toby did.

Sue, the night nurse, arrived at 10pm and bent over Ronnie. I was in the living room. Fifteen minutes after her arrival she called me into his room as his breathing died quietly away.

At that exact second when his breath failed, I like to think that the trumpets (or perhaps Royal Marine bugles) started sounding on the other side for him. In his own way, like all good journalists, Ronnie had been valiant for truth.

Those last three days with him had been special for me. I look back and feel they were some of the most precious days of my life with him.

Postscript

Love is stronger than death – so are kittens

I'd done it. I hadn't failed him. My greatest fear, that I would let him down at the end and fail to give him a good death, had been unfounded. I'd had the good fun when he was in health and I'd had the bad times at his side right to the end when he was in sickness. I had been faithful at the end of our marriage. I had made amends for my time as a really bad wife. He had died well and I had helped him in his last achievement.

The house martins that had been building a nest in my porch deserted it on the very day Ronnie died. Too many people – nurses, doctors, paramedics and funeral directors – had been coming and going. They never came back to the porch. I felt that they were a symbol of Ronnie's leaving me never to return. It was as if they had accompanied his spirit. It comforted me, even though I know that nature is indifferent to the fate of all living beings.

I have wondered why he chose to die naturally rather than taking his own life. Why not go early instead of having those last miserable weeks, when his life had so much diminished? I had been ready to help him if that had been his decision. I asked one of his friends.

'I think he would have seen it as his duty not to kill himself,' said the friend. 'He would have seen it as his duty to go on to the last.'

This made sense to me. At his core, Ronnie was still, so many years later, a Royal Marine. Once a marine, always a marine.

Toby and Tilly had accepted the new and different regime without any fuss whatsoever. I had meant to show them Ronnie's body before it was taken away the following morning. I thought it might explain his disappearance to them. But in the night, while the body, a mere thing, lay waiting for collection, I had forgotten to do this. Instead, later that morning I put both cats, one after the other, on the hospital bed, to show them that there was now no Ronnie there.

I hadn't given either of them much attention during those last days of his life, and perhaps because of that they were particularly affectionate to me. Two days after his death, I went to bed for the afternoon. I was exhausted. Toby joined me sitting very close to me, almost (but not quite – he had his pride!) in my arms. Then sometime while I was asleep, Tilly came, too – the other side of me and lower down the bed. I woke to two cats lying amicably on the same bed – not friends, of course, but acquaintances, who would tolerate each other.

There was a setback for Toby, shortly after Ronnie's death. In the evening, at the cats' normal eating time, he was absent. I checked every room in case he had somehow got himself shut in a cupboard. Then I walked round the garden calling for him. Thanks to the target training, he would usually come when called. No Toby. Tilly wandered round with me, worried by my behaviour, rather than his absence.

I felt devastated. I had lost Ronnie forever and now it looked as if I had lost Toby. He wasn't the sort of cat that went on long patrols. True, he had got used to the garden but he hadn't yet ventured into the fields. Then I remembered the garage. I had shut him in by mistake. He came out chastened and anxious. His reaction was to revert to even more clinging behaviour around me.

I decided I must help him explore his wider environment. Where I went, Toby would follow, so I escorted him into the wider world. I took him to prime mousing territory, behind the nearby barn where William used to catch mice in front of my very eyes and where Tilly stalked rabbits. I sat in the long grass on this patch of ground in the evening sun. Tilly wandered round, taking in the scents of mice and rabbits. Toby just frolicked. He ran up and down, jumped about and generally behaved like a kitten. The smell of mice and rabbits seemed of no interest to him.

Next I took him down the track to the nearest field. He followed me trustfully, like a dog. He didn't seem very interested in the surroundings, just in my company. Tilly hunted along the side of the track, looking for mice. Toby remained glued to my side. Having introduced him to a wider world, I took him back, trailing after me, towards the house.

Inside the house, both cats were taking the changes in their stride. They hadn't particularly liked the invalid equipment that Ronnie had needed so were not concerned when I slowly got rid of it. The hospital bed, the special chair and his walking frames were collected by the agency that had supplied them. I went back to sleep in the comfortable double bed in our bedroom instead of on the uncomfortable sofa in the living room.

Each change from the old punishing routine and its equipment should have been a relief. Not so. Each change took me further away from Ronnie.

The chair lift that once had allowed Ronnie upstairs had to be collected by the supplier's engineer. The day before he arrived to dismantle it, I was in the garden and heard a squeak and a scuffle in the shrubs. This had to be something to do with Tilly, as Toby was in plain sight. I thought little of it.

Half an hour later I went back into the house. Cowering near the front door with two cats peering somewhat doubtfully at him was a young rat. When I walked in, he made a run for the stair lift and disappeared into its workings. Both cats ran up and down stairs peering over the rail that attached the chair to the wall.

Then they lost interest and strolled off. I have always found this sudden loss of interest strange. A cat that has waited by a mouse hole for three or four hours, caught an emerging mouse, brought it into the house and let it go will then walk away. Inexplicable behaviour.

I can bear the presence of living mice in my house, but rats are quite another matter. I wasn't sure where exactly this rat was hiding. I hoped it was still in the stair lift rail but perhaps it had run upstairs within the rail and was now in a bedroom.

Possibly *my* bedroom. In the middle of mourning Ronnie, I had a rat in my bedroom. At this moment, I remember thinking that if the choice was between feeling grief or feeling fear of rats I would prefer grief.

I did what the cats had done. I just strolled away. I went to see friends for a couple of hours and returned to find both cats in the garden. The little beggars had just left the rat to roam around in the house.

The cats followed me indoors and at this very moment, by sheer chance, the rat emerged from the stair lift workings on to the stairs. Toby pounced on him and paraded around the house with the rat in his mouth. His head was held high with pride in his prey. I managed to shoo him out into the garden with the rat still securely in his jaws. On his way out he gave a mew that suggested to me the rat may have bitten him, but, luckily, he did not drop it.

He ran off, pursued by Tilly. I shut all doors and the cat flap, so neither cats nor rat could come in. Twenty minutes later, both cats demanded to come in. I watched TV lying on the sofa and both cats joined me, sleeping on top of me, exhausted with their happy time of hunting. I did not know the fate of the rat.

Without the cats to divert me, whether with pleasure in or horror at their rodent slaughter, my life now consisted of sleep, both at night and in the afternoons, three-hour walks with a walking group, and paperwork. Tilly woke me in the mornings to make sure I got up in time, and both of them greeted me when I returned to the house. Toby reminded me when it was time to take him and his food up to his bedroom for the night.

Their loving presence – albeit of the cupboard-love type – helped me slip into an ordinary daily routine. It was strange to have lost the focus of care on Ronnie. Each morning I prayed to a God, some Higher Power that I did not always believe in, to care for Ronnie since I no longer could do so. Luckily for me, I still had two personalities to care for – one furry, brown, small with a slightly weeping eye; one furry, large and ginger with acne, waxy ears and cross eyes. They needed me and I certainly needed them.

Better still, the next month I had a kitten to foster.

Sweetie had been found starving and blind in a local market town, where Annie rescues cats. She had picked up this little tortoiseshell and white kitten on a patch of wasteland where it had been dumped. The kitten was starving and ill, with eyes so swollen that they were completely closed. Sweetie, as I found myself calling her, needed two days at the veterinary clinic just to recover from dehydration, lack of food and chlamydia. The vet operated on her to open up her closed eyes.

As Annie already had more than her share of rescued cats waiting for a home, I picked up Sweetie from the vet's and took her home. She was wet all over because she had rolled in her water. She had to have ear drops twice a day and eye drops three times daily. Annie said she had been as good as gold two days before. The veterinary nurses said she was 'lively'.

'Lively' turned out to be a code word for terrified. I had prepared my dog crate and put her in it. She immediately wriggled through the bars and out into the dining room. I tried to pick her up and she bit me. Even small kittens with tiny kitten teeth can manage a painful bite if they get you in the quick of the nail. She did.

Sweetie disappeared underneath a cupboard. I watched her through the glass door between the living room and Ronnie's old bedroom, where I had put her. She came out briefly to eat. She was still obviously hungry. Then she flung herself in desperation at the French windows trying to get out. Either she did not know about glass or her sight was dim and she couldn't see the glass. Then she retreated back underneath the cupboard.

I edged her out with a soft broom, and stuffed blankets underneath the cupboard so she couldn't get back there. I could not leave her there to come out of her own accord because I had to administer the eye and ear drops prescribed by the vet. By now, a proper kitten crate had arrived from a fellow Sunshine Cat Rescue volunteer. I put her inside it. The little mite was shaking with fear when I picked her up.

Weak from starvation on the wasteland, she had been easily handled by her original rescuer, Annie. Maybe the operation to separate her eyelids had traumatized her, or perhaps her fear was partly my fault. I am not as good at handling cats as I might be. Dog behaviourists get handling experience at dog-training classes. There are no training classes for cats. They just wouldn't work.

Toby and Tilly watched the tiny intruder with fascination through the glass door. In Tilly's case the fascination was mixed with horror! Both cats wanted to come in and take a closer look but because Sweetie had chlamydia she had to remain in quarantine to protect them from infection. I had fostered several adult cats before but Sweetie was the first kitten I had cared for in this way.

The little creature that I was helping survive was helping me survive the cold numbness of loss that had settled on my mind. In the midst of Ronnie's death, there was cat life.

After the trauma of the first day, Sweetie settled down.

I could take her out in the morning to put drops in her eyes and in her ears. Naturally, she hated this procedure – most cats do. I had to wrap her in a towel in order to put her in a position where I could get the drops in.

I decided to hand feed some of her breakfast to her and her hunger began to overcome her fear of me. After about a tablespoonful, she even purred a little. I let her eat the rest inside her kitten crate, but I could tell she was not happy in confinement. She blundered about the cage and still tried to get out. I administered some more drops and fed her off my hand at lunchtime.

She purred all the way through the food, but when I put her back in the crate, she stumbled into the water bowl. It looked as if she might be partially blind. There was water everywhere. I reorganized the cage, moving the water bowl, but to no avail. She was using the litter tray but trying to dig a hole the size of a Colditz escape tunnel. There was litter everywhere, much of it in the water bowl. I tried a litter tray with higher sides, also to no avail. I decided that the problem was mostly that she hated being caged. It was probably her desperate escape efforts that were making her upset the water, tear up the newspaper on the floor of the kitten crate and spill litter everywhere.

Each time I took her out of the cage, we would have a little love fest. By the end of her third day, it was clear that she enjoyed being stroked. For a tiny, sick kitten she had a powerful purr. She would even roll on her back for me – the social roll that cats sometimes use to get human attention – and I could tickle her tummy without her feeling anxious. She was a tough little survivor but also a loving one.

In her past, humans had clearly handled, stroked and loved her. Yet these same humans had chucked her out like a piece of rubbish when she became ill, leaving her to die slowly on the streets. Was it because they could not afford vet's fees? Or was it just that a kitten was like a toy to them, to be discarded when broken?

I decided she would thrive better out of the kitten cage, and so she did. Being shut in a small space had worried her. Now she used the kitten cage for the litter tray, and once her food and water were given to her elsewhere, she no longer needed to spread water everywhere.

It took several days, more vet visits and more medication before her eyes healed. With regular meals she became playful and while I was in the living room with Toby and Tilly, I would hear noises from the next-door room as she played with her toys.

Both her eyes healed, although one was still slightly less open than the other. She could see, though I am not sure if both eyes had perfect sight. She had her vaccinations and for the first time I let her into the living room where she could get accustomed to the TV and (I hoped) to the other cats.

It was not a success.

Tilly saw the intruder and immediately left the room. Toby strolled in and at first all seemed to go well. He was greeted by her with various jumps and sideways-on displays (with her back up to show her at full height) – signs of playful aggression mixed with anxiousness. She jumped up and down with all four feet in the air. She greeted him nose to nose. Then she crept up on him and batted his fluffy tail.

Despite being four or five times her size, Toby looked distinctly anxious. He lay down (probably so as to have his four paws ready for defence if needed). Then, still anxious, he decided to get up again. Then he lay down again. Sweetie jumped around, dashed up to him and biffed him, dashed away, came up very close and biffed him again. Then, with his tail down, his ears back and looking very upset indeed, Toby slunk unhappily out of the living room.

Toby, the cat who bullied Tilly, had been bullied in his turn by a ten-week-old kitten. I'm afraid I laughed.

The next time I let him in the room with her, much the same thing happened. After finishing a few fragments of her food, Toby thought he might be undisturbed if he sat on the armchair. He was mistaken. Sweetie jumped from the top of an adjoining chair to the top of his chair, then simply flung herself downwards on to the seat beside him. Discomforted by this behaviour, he left the chair.

Next she started biffing him from under the chair. He biffed back but with his claws sheathed. After more harassment he gave me a plaintive look, so I opened the door and he slunk out.

Game, set and match to Sweetie.

Clearly, she was not going to be sociable to other cats. So once she had been spayed, she was rehomed as a single cat. A smart young man, wearing an expensive striped shirt and impeccable business suit, turned up to collect her. I could see he was impatient to take her away and get to know her on his own. He looked like a man ready to fall in love.

Sweetie shamed me by refusing to let me pick her up, so I had to bribe her into the carrier with cat biscuits. I gave her new owner a strip of blanket with her smell, some used not-quite-clean litter with her smell, and some kitten food. I was delaying the moment of departure. I didn't want to lose her.

Finally, I warned him that she had the heart of a lion in her tiny body, she might attack other cats with no idea of her own safety and, in general, there was a huge personality in that scrap of a cat. He drove off down the track with her. I felt confident that she would be able to wrap him round her little paw. Such a tough little cat would be training him into a good human pet in no time at all.

Toby was thrilled by her absence. He walked round the two rooms, making sure that the aggressive little intruder had really gone. Then he settled back on his chair. Tilly, far more cautious by nature, took several weeks before she would come back into the room at all.

The wearying business of the income-tax authorities, probate, changing utility direct debits, closing bank accounts came and went. I decided I should go out and learn how to trap cats with our local expert trapper. In August, when people go on holiday, some of them just dump their cats rather than making feeding arrangements. Others chuck out elderly or sick cats that need veterinary treatment, and still others dump kittens they cannot sell.

I met Sophie, my next foster kitten, in this way. She was one of two kittens wandering about a local housing estate, being fed occasionally by cat lovers. By the time the trapper from Sunshine Cat Rescue and I arrived, one of the kittens had disappeared, perhaps run over by a car one night. The other, the little tabby Sophie, went into the trap quite easily.

A few weeks later, after I had been on holiday, Sophie arrived at my house to be fostered. She had been brought up on the streets, we thought, so we didn't know how tame she might become. The first five hours she spent frozen with terror on the litter tray in the kitten cage. Then she transferred herself to the kitten bed, used the tray for both sorts of elimination, but was still too terrified to eat. I left her with food overnight and she ate it.

When I opened the cage door, she disappeared under the sideboard and refused to come out if I was in the room. It seemed likely that she might have had very little human handling.

By sheer chance I discovered the way to entice her out. Toby had followed me into the room without my noticing him, and as soon as she saw him, out she came. She fell in love with him immediately. She rolled on her back, tried to twine tails with him, rubbed against the chair while looking amorously at him, rubbed up against his flank – all the signs of a kitten with a passion for an older tom. Toby ignored her in a condescending way or swiped very gently with a paw when she was too insistent.

To get her used to coming out from her hiding place, I fed Toby his breakfast in her room while she was also being fed. Thanks to his intervention, she would sometimes emerge for me, too, if I used a fishing-rod toy! Once, while she was swooping past Toby (who was thoughtfully cleaning up her food bowl) I even managed to put a gentle finger on her back. She flinched slightly but didn't disappear under the sideboard.

She needed to get used to a human home, so I let her into the living room as soon as possible and left the TV on when I went out. I petted Toby in front of her, so that she might see his behaviour and imitate it.

I bought some high-quality dry kitten food, which I used to lure her closer. Soon she would eat about 18 inches away from me, but she would be looking up at me all the time, and backed off if I moved. However, I found that with the new dry kitten food I could feed her piece by piece at lunchtime nearer her bowl until, eventually, she would eat it out of my hand.

From then onwards, all her food was given to her by hand. Sophie tamed surprisingly quickly. I could hold out my hand and she would rub against it. She would even lie on her back and let me tickle her tummy, and she would come up to me for a stroke. Toby had set a good example.

The next stage was to teach her to sit on my knee while I was watching TV. Thanks to her desire for food, there was no difficulty about this. I hand fed her while I watched and then she would lie on her back on my lap and let me stroke her tummy. But if I ever tried to pick her up, she dashed away. At some stage in her life, Sophie had been traumatized when somebody had picked her up.

She continued to admire, even worship, Toby. If he came in to sit on his chair while I watched TV, she would jump up and join him rather than sit with me. Then she would groom his head for several minutes, holding him down with one paw. He enjoyed this so much that his eyes would close with pleasure and he would go into a kind of trance.

Then, unfortunately, her affection would overwhelm her and she would give him a love bite that obviously hurt, at which point he would jump off the chair. It was as if she could not help going too far. He never retaliated when she hurt him, nor could he resist her grooming, even though he must have known how it might end.

To take Sophie to the vet for her vaccinations and to be spayed, I had just picked her up when she was being stroked and wasn't expecting it, and quickly put her in the cat carrier. Now I trained her to enter the carrier of her own accord by putting food inside for her to find. She went in to search for the food, and I shut the door on her. It was that simple.

Toby had turned out to be the perfect kitten nanny. Tilly, on the other hand, continued to avoid the kitten intruder. Her look of disgust if she saw the kitten through the glass door, was comical. When a vaccinated, spayed and microchipped Sophie went to her new home, I decided I would not regularly foster kittens, but take the occasional one who needed special care. I did not want Tilly to be permanently stressed by a stream of unwanted kittens.

Sweetie and Sophie had brought new joy into my life that summer – small, simple joys in the bleak landscape of losing Ronnie. Part of my heart has been amputated by Ronnie's death. I have no choice but to lead a new and different life without him but at least Toby and Tilly are still with me.

If there is a heaven where we shall meet again, I hope there will be cats there. Any personal heaven would have to have my beloved cats as well as Ronnie – Moppet, Fat Ada, Little Mog, William, George, Tilly and Toby. It wouldn't be heaven otherwise.

Like Ronnie, I have an uncertain hope in some kind of afterlife. I pray daily and tell Ronnie I am on the journey towards him. Even if there is only an eternal nothingness, then I will be with him and the cats again in that nothingness.

Thanks

My last book, *Tilly the Ugliest Cat in the Shelter*, should have included thanks to Gordon Wise, who was wonderful, truly wonderful, in the darkest moments of my life. Thanks to Trevor Davies of Octopus who kept me on the right lines for the book and is a fellow cat lover; to surgeon Mr Michael Greenall, who had to put up with my combative attitude; and to Richard Medland, Exmoor walk guide (*www.exmoorwalkguide.co.uk*), who somehow walked me out of fear and into acceptance.

Here are some of the other people who helped Ronnie and me in the last five years of Ronnie's life – Simon and Nikki, Jeannette, Martin and Anne, Stella, Tracy, Brian, John and Vivien, Adrian and Claire, Jane and Martin, Tim, Jane (who inexplicably hates cats but is otherwise terrific), community nurse Caroline and Helen the community nurse who visited Ronnie in his last days, Lizzie the palliative nurse, Kate's nursing team, all the Heart to Heart carers, and, of course, my family.

Thanks to Ronnie's friends who visited him, had lunch with him or invited him to stay while he was ill. And, of course, all my friends in Carterton, Cirencester and Burford, who helped me stay sober and more or less sane. A special thank you to Noreen, who made me laugh at the worst moment of all.

Helpful organizations
Cat stuff

My own website at www.catexpert.co.uk has lots of free information about cat behaviour – and, as it happens, information on the behaviour of rabbits, hamsters and guinea pigs. I also do cat behaviour consultations in the West Oxfordshire area. Contact me via the website.

Association of Pet Behaviour Counsellors has a list of pet behaviourists at www.apbc.org.uk

Cats Protection at www.cats.org.uk is the largest cat charity in the UK and a good source of information on all sorts of cat issues. Tilly was rescued by Cats Protection.

Coape Association of Pet Behaviourists and Trainers If you have a problem cat, you can get a behaviourist here: www.capbt.org

Finstock Cattery, West Oxfordshire The cattery doesn't have a website. Its email is finstockcattery@aol.com

International Cat Care at www.icatcare.org has reliable information on almost all cat problems and diseases. It also offers online courses on cat welfare that can be done from anywhere in the world.

Sunshine Cat Rescue Sweetie and Sophie found their forever homes through this small West Oxfordshire charity. It really does need help, so if you can spare a few pounds, please make a donation via the website at www.sunshinecatrescue.org.uk using Paypal.

People stuff

Amazon There is some information about me and a list of my books at www.amazon.co.uk/Celia-Haddon/e/B001K8EQKG

Alcoholics Anonymous for help with a drinking problem. The worldwide official site is www.aa.org, while the UK site is www.alcoholics-anonymous.org.uk

Blog My late cat George lives on at his blog – you can find it at online at www.george-online.blogspot.com. He is a qualified pet human behaviour expert and gives advice on the behaviour of *Homo sapiens* (which he considers a misnomer).

Centre of Applied Pet Ethology at www.coape.co.uk is a good place to find courses if you want to learn more about dogs and cats. Also look at International Cat Care (see previous page) for courses on boarding and breeding cats.

Facebook I have an open Facebook page where I put photos of Tilly and Toby at www.facebook.com/CeliaHaddonBooks I also put any book news there.

Gaynor the Trainer and cake maker can be found at www. gaynor-the-trainer.co.uk If you want a gorgeous novelty cake, and live in Oxfordshire, contact her there.

Twitter You can find me on Twitter by simply googling Twitter – Celia Haddon. At the time of writing, this is *twitter. com/TillyUgliestCat* but I might change it and give Toby a chance to tweet.

Celia Haddon is a renowned pet journalist and was for many years the *Daily Telegraph*'s pet agony aunt. Her best-selling books include *Tilly: The Ugliest Cat in the Shelter*, and her humorous book *One Hundred Ways for a Cat to Train its Human* has sold over a quarter of a million copies worldwide.

For free information about cat behaviour problems, visit Celia's website at www.celiahaddon.com